MW00780082

SELF-STEERING UNDER SAIL

Autopilots and Wind-steering Systems

Peter Christian Förthmann

INTERNATIONAL MARINE
Camden, Maine

0486

Bibliography

Selfsteering for Sailing Craft, JS Letcher jr, International Marine Publishing, Camden, Maine, USA.
Selfsteering, The Amateur Yacht Research Society, Woodacres, Hythe, Kent, UK.
Cruising under Sail, Eric Hiscock, Adlard Coles Nautical, London, UK, and International Marine Publishing, Camden, Maine, USA.
Windvaan stuur inrichtingen, Gerard Dijkstra, De Boer Maritim, Unieboek BV Bossum, Amsterdam.
Pen Duick, Eric Tabarly, Adlard Coles Nautical, London, UK.
Windsteueranlagen, Volz/Molu, Verlag Klasing & Co, Bielefeld, Germany.
Barrer sans Barreur, Jean Philippe Malice, Editions Maritimes et d'outre-mer, Paris.
Selbststeueranlagen, Gerard Dijkstra, Verlag Delius Klasing & Co, Bielefeld, Germany.
Around the World Rally, Jimmy Cornell, Adlard Coles Nautical London, UK, and Sheridan House Inc, New York, USA.
World Cruising Survey, Jimmy Cornell, Adlard Coles Nautical, London, UK, and International Marine Publishing, Camden, Maine, USA.

Illustration acknowlegments

P ii Kai Greiser, Hamburg; pp 7, 14, 17 Raytheon UK/Navico UK; pp 11/13 Simrad, Norway; p 12 Gert Fopma, Netherlands; pp 40, 41 Derek Daniels UK; pp 50, 133 Hans Bernwall, USA; p 126 Nick Franklin, UK; p 130 Paul Visser, Netherlands; p 139 Brian Mereloo, UK.

Title and all other photos: Peter Christian Förthmann, Germany.
Line drawings: Jörg Peter Kusserow, Germany.

Title page illustration: At the helm – work or pleasure?

Published in the USA by International Marine.

Copyright © Peter Christian Förthmann 1998

First published in Germany by Paul Pietsch Verlage Stuttgart under the title *Autopiloten und Windsteuersysteme*

Published in Great Britain in 1998 by Adlard Coles Nautical, an imprint of A & C Black Ltd.

Translated by Chris Sandison

ISBN 0-07-022011-5

A CIP catalog record for this book is available from the Library of Congress.

Typeset in Palatino and Frutiger by Eric Drewery Design

Printed and bound in Spain by GZ Printek, Bilbao

Contents

Foreword

For some strange reason, most cruising sailors profoundly dislike steering by hand. The prospect of spending hour after hour at the helm used to deter most people from long-distance cruising. This is undoubtedly the main reason why, until relatively recently, the number of sailing boats venturing far afield was very small indeed. However, all that changed with the advent of automatic pilots specifically built for yachts plus the development of efficient wind operated self-steering devices. Suddenly, the chore of hand-steering was a thing of the past and long ocean passages could be a pleasure – even on yachts with the smallest of crews. Having made one circumnavigation of over 70,000 miles with an Aries and another of some 40,000 miles with a Hydrovane, I could not be accused of exaggerating if I state unreservedly that one of the most important pieces of equipment on any cruising yacht is a wind-operated self-steering gear.

Unfortunately, and surprisingly, this view is not shared by many cruising sailors. This is primarily because as most of us have grown up with technology around us, we tend to take the push-button mentality with us to sea. Steering a given course is easy to achieve by setting a compass course and pushing a button on the autopilot, and, nowadays, this is what most sailors prefer to do. It is usually on the first morning with flat batteries that the love-affair with their favourite toy comes to an abrupt end. Having been forced to listen to countless heart-rending stories on this very theme at the end of the ARC or similar trans-ocean rally, I managed to persuade Peter Förthmann to come to Las Palmas before the start of the ARC to talk to our participants about the pros and cons of self-steering. His talks and workshops became an instant success, not only because he knows this subject better than anyone else in the world, but also because he always speaks generically about both wind-operated self-steering gears and electronic autopilots. He never tried to sell his own products and, in this way, enjoyed the interest and confidence of his audience.

I am therefore pleased, not only that he took my advice to write this long-overdue book, but also that he managed to do it so fairly and objectively by giving all his competitors an equal opportunity to make their products known. All existing systems are described in the following pages, allowing the reader to make up his own mind. Many sailors agree that Peter's Windpilot is currently the best gear available. Being both the inventor and manufacturer of this ingenious device, Peter has indeed shown that his name should stand alongside those of his great precursors: Blondie Hasler, Marcel Gianoli, Nick Franklin. This book confirms Peter Förthmann's standing as the world authority on wind-operated self-steering gears.

Jimmy Cornell

Preface

Whoever would have thought that the world could change so much in a single generation?

Yachts which were so recently state of the art are suddenly dated, their technology surpassed. The range of instrumentation and equipment available to the sailor has expanded beyond all belief; on-board GPS, EPIRB, INMARSAT, chart plotter, radar and Internet access are now all but taken for granted. The market for nautical books has also been very fertile. Every topic has been explored, every hitherto mysterious subject laid bare. Hard to believe, then, that the theme of this book has been neglected for a whole generation!

A book on self-steering systems has been long overdue. That, at least, was the feeling of Jimmy Cornell, whose encouragement finally convinced me to take up my pen. It was a decision not lightly taken, for there can hardly be a more sensitive topic for a manufacturer of windvane steering systems. But, equally, there can hardly be a better one, since few topics in sailing are as logical and intuitive. All self-steering systems rely on the same physical principles; here there is no wizardry and no impenetrable mire of theory.

This book, I hope, will cut through the tangle of conflicting opinions and contradictory hearsay surrounding the subject of self-steering. If it saves you the disappointment of a self-steering failure and the exhaustion of hours at the helm in cold, dark and stormy seas, it will have achieved its aim. If it exposes gaps in your understanding, or flaws in your own self-steering solution, take heart; it is far better to see your mistakes now, safe in harbour, than half way across the ocean. Once at sea you must live with the hand you have dealt yourself; cold comfort as with heavy arms and tired eyes you turn the wheel once more and stare off into the distance wishing that you did not still have such a long, long way to go...

I would like to give particular thanks to the following people:

Jimmy Cornell, whose words 'you sit down and start writing' I can still hear today!

Jörg Peter Kusserow, my friend and business partner without whose illustrations this book would be a great deal poorer.

Chris Sandison, who found a way to translate my language into yours.

Janet Murphy of Adlard Coles Nautical, who kept on smiling as the mountain of paper continued to rise.

And a final thanks to you the reader, if you find this book leaves you wiser as to how to make your sailing easier – without staying ashore!

Peter Christian Förthmann

Introduction

Throughout human history people have been taking to the water in sailing boats, be it for trade, exploration or war. Not until the twentieth century, though, did the idea first surface that a sailing boat might be able to steer itself. In the heyday of the tall ships, and even well into the modern era, steering meant hands on the wheel. Crew were plentiful and cheap, and all the work on deck, in the rigging or with the anchor was performed manually. Where brute force was insufficient there were blocks and tackle, cargo runners and, for the anchor, the mechanical advantage of long bars and a capstan. Some of the last generation of tall ships, engaged in their losing battle with the expanding steamship fleet, did carry small steam-powered engines to assist the crew, but steering nevertheless remained a strictly manual task. There were three steering watches and the work was hard – even lashing the helm with a warp helped considerably. The great square-riggers plied the oceans without the help of electric motors or hydraulic systems.

In the early part of the twentieth century, recreational sailing was the preserve of the elite. Yachting was a sport for wealthy owners with large crews, and nobody would have dreamed of allowing the 'prime' position on board, the helm, to be automated.

It was only after the triumph of steam, and the ensuing rapid increase in international trade and travel, that the human helmsperson gradually became unnecessary; the first autopilot was invented in 1950.

Powerful electrohydraulic autopilots were soon part of the standard equipment on every new ship, and although the wheel was retained, it now came to be positioned to the side of the increasingly important automatic controls. Commercial ships and fishing boats quickly adapted electric or hydraulic systems to just about every task above and below deck – from loading gear, anchor capstans and cargo hatch controls to winches for net recovery and making fast. Before long ships had become complex systems of electric generators and consumers, and as long as the main engine was running there was power in abundance.

Today, the world's commercial and fishing fleets are steered exclusively by autopilots – a fact that should give every blue water sailor pause for thought. Even the most alert watchperson on the bridge of a container ship at 22 knots is powerless to prevent it from ploughing ahead a little longer before gently turning to one side. A freighter on the horizon comes up quickly, particularly since the height of eye on a sailing yacht is virtually zero. Collisions between sailing boats and container ships, as immortalised in the cartoons of Mike Peyton, prey on the mind of every sailor. Horror stories appear time and again in the yachting magazines, and in almost all of them the sailing boat ends up sleeping with the fish. Sometimes the sailors are rescued and the story has a happy ending. The tale of one solo sailor whose yacht inadvertently turned the tables on the merchant fleet by spearing a fishing cutter while he was sleeping caught the attention of the daily press all around the world. As sensational as it is unique, this incident involved the courts as well.

It is tempting on these grounds to condemn singlehanded sailing as highly dangerous – after all, the skipper has to sleep sooner or later. All too easily overlooked, however, is the fact that commercial vessels the world over are regularly entrusted to a lone pair of eyes on long night watches ... and if they should fall shut, the end result is the same: a ghost ship and great danger for any unfortunate seafarer who strays into the wrong place at the wrong time.

The human helm's time at sea is just about up; not only tireless and more reliable, but often more competent as well, the iron helm is making the hand on the tiller all but superfluous. Even through the narrowest straits off the coast of Sweden, Stena Line's large ferries navigate every rock and shoal at full speed with only an autopilot and the Decca pulses of their purpose-designed software at the helm. All that remains for the sailor is a supervisory role – a role which, of course, you can only carry out for as long as your eyes stay open!

Steering the Russian square-rigger *Sedov.*

· 1 ·

The history of self-steering

Shorthanded long-distance sailing started with just a few hardy pioneers – Joshua Slocum was one of the very first with his legendary *Spray*. It is said he could keep the boat on a fairly steady course using an ingenious sheeting arrangement or simply by lashing fast the wheel. This manner of self-steering willingly sacrificed a certain amount of sail power to free up a portion of the sail area just for steering trim. Of course, *Spray* had a natural tendency to sail straight, as her keel was almost as long as her waterline.

Hambley Tregoning described in a letter to *Yachting Monthly* in 1919 how the tiller of a boat could be connected to a windvane. Upon publication of his letter, owners of model boats rushed out to fit their craft with wind-guided steering. They found they could achieve admirable results with even the most simple mechanical connection between the tiller and a windvane. This type of system did not transfer very successfully, though, since the forces generated by a windvane are too small to move the tiller of a full-size vessel directly.

The first windvane steering system

The first windvane steering system, rather ironically, was installed on a motorboat. Frenchman Marin Marie used an oversized windvane connected to the rudder by lines to steer the 14 m/46 ft motor yacht *Arielle* during his spectacular 18-day singlehanded crossing from New York to Le Havre in 1936. His windvane steering system is now on display at the Musée de la Marine in Port Louis.

British sailor Ian Major took *Buttercup* singlehanded from Europe to the Antilles in 1955 using a small windvane to control a trim tab mounted on the main rudder. This was the most common system in the early days of windvane steering. It was also in 1955 when Englishman Michael Henderson fitted a personal creation, nicknamed 'Harriet, the third hand', to his famous 17-footer *Mick the Miller*. His approach was to centre the main rudder and use the windvane to move a small, additional rudder blade. The system was a complete success and was able to handle more than half the steering duties.

Bernard Moitessier also chose a trim tab for *Marie Thérèse II* in 1957, and used a simplified version of the same system on *Joshua* from 1965 onwards. In this second version, the windvane was fastened directly to the shaft of the trim tab.

The starting gun of the first OSTAR (Observer Singlehanded

Transatlantic Race) in Plymouth on 11 June 1960 signalled the real beginning of the windvane steering era. Without some form of self-steering, none of the five participants – Francis Chichester, Blondie Hasler, David Lewis, Valentine Howells and Jean Lacombe – could have reached the finish.

Francis Chichester's first windvane gear, christened 'Miranda', consisted of an oversized windvane (almost $4\,m^2/43\,ft^2$) and a $12\,kg/26\frac{1}{2}\,lb$ counterweight, and was connected directly to the tiller via lines and turning blocks. However, the giant windvane turned out to have anarchic tendencies, and Chichester was soon contemplating a change to the windvane/rudder proportions.

Aboard *Jester*, Blondie Hasler was using the first servo-pendulum gear with differential gearing. David Lewis and Valentine Howells both used simple trim tab systems driven directly by a windvane. Jean Lacombe used a trim tab gear, developed jointly with Marcel Gianoli,

Hasler servo-pendulum system on an Sparkman & Stephens 30.

which had a variable transmission ratio.

Hasler and Gianoli, an Englishman and a Frenchman, were to play a significant role in the development of windvane steering systems. The principles they established are still used today, and we will consider both their systems later on.

The second OSTAR was held in 1964. Once again, all the competitors used windvane steering systems, with six of them opting for servo-pendulum gears built by Hasler, who had already undertaken a small production run. Windvane steering gears were virtually standard equipment for the 1966 and 1970 Round Britain Races as well, for electric autopilots were still banned.

The field for the 1972 OSTAR was so large that the organisers had to set an entry cap of 100 boats for the 1976 race. Electric autopilots were allowed, but could not be powered by inboard motors or generators. By now, many of the participants were using professionally built windvane steering gears. There were 12 from Hasler, 10 from Atoms, 6 from Aries, 4 from Gunning, 2 from QME, 2 electric, 2 auxiliary rudder gears, 2 from Quartermaster and 1 Hasler trim tab. The rise of the great solo and short-handed blue water races, none of which would have been feasible without windvane gear, stimulated the professional development and construction of a wide range of different systems in England, France, Italy and Germany. The early pioneers are still familiar names: Hasler, Aries, Atoms, Gunning, QME and Windpilot.

Several factors contributed to the rapid spread of windvane steering systems, in particular the economic miracle of the post-war years, the increasing number of series-built sailing boats, and the shift in boat-building away from one-at-a-time construction in wood towards mass production with modern materials. Sailing was no longer a sport for obsessive loners or the elite, and its popularity was growing.

The first companies producing professionally designed and built windvane steering systems appeared in Britain, France and Germany in 1968, and soon after in the Netherlands. The following lists the windvane steering systems by the year they were launched:

1962: Blondie Hasler, **Hasler**
1962: Marcel Gianoli, **MNOP**
1968: John Adam, **Windpilot**
1968: Pete Beard, **QME**
1968: Nick Franklin, **Aries**
1970: Henri Brun, **Atoms**
1970: Derek Daniels, **Hydrovane**
1972: Charron/Waché, **Navik**
1976: Boström/Knöös, **Sailomat**

The first cockpit autopilot

The first electric autopilots on non-commercial vessels probably appeared in the United States. The first Tillermaster, a miniaturised autopilot developed for small fishing boats, was produced in 1970.

British engineer Derek Fawcett, formerly employed at Lewmar, launched his Autohelm brand in 1974. Autohelm soon dominated the world market, with its small push rod models being particularly successful. The systems were manufactured in large production runs by a workforce that quickly expanded to 200.

· 2 ·

Windvane steering systems versus autopilots

Our aim in this book is to investigate the functioning and the pros and cons of the various systems, and to help the reader decide which is most suitable for his or her particular needs. The two main categories of self-steering system are the autopilot and the windvane steering gear. Autopilots are electro-mechanical systems that obtain their steering impulse from a compass, whereas windvane gears use wind and water power and obtain their steering impulse from the apparent wind angle. We will consider each in turn.

A sailing yacht generates all its drive from the position of the boat and the orientation of the sails with respect to the wind; trim the sails poorly and there will be no drive. This simple relationship explains why a windvane gear is ideal for steering a sailing yacht. The wind angle it uses is exactly that which gives the boat drive; set this angle once, and drive is assured. The benefits of steering to the apparent wind angle are particularly pronounced when sailing to weather. Even the slightest shift in the wind is immediately translated into a course change and optimum drive is ensured – a degree of sensitivity beyond even the best human helm.

Why autopilots?

Put simply, autopilots are compact and discreet. When it comes to buying a self-steering system, probably the largest single factor counting against windvane gears is their incongruous appearance. They are generally large and bulky – hardly the ideal transom ornament. Not only that, but some are also rather unwieldy and heavy and tend to get in the way when manoeuvring in harbour under engine.

Autopilots, by contrast, are virtually invisible in the cockpit and may even be completely concealed below deck. Once installed they are simple to operate, only requiring mastery of a few buttons. Cockpit autopilots are light and generally inexpensive and they steer a compass course. For some sailors this argument is compelling; autopilots were programmed to succeed.

Over many years the sailing world has polarised into two camps. In the 1970s windvane steering systems became a common sight on blue water yachts, where they were indispensable. Only in exceptional cases were they to be seen on holiday and weekend boats (and some of these can almost certainly be put down to wishful thinking!).

This 65 foot Koopmans is steered by both autopilot and windvane gear.

There has been heated debate over the last 25 years between advocates of the two different systems. One particular bone of contention was the repeated insistence by some that vessels of several tonnes or more are 'easily' steered with just fractions of an ampere. Views today are more realistic. There is no getting around the laws of physics: every desired 'output' (steering force) requires a certain 'input' (current/ energy). Who could forget the 'Conservation of Energy' law so familiar from school physics lessons?

· *3* ·

Autopilots

How they work

Autopilots depend on a compass. A steering impulse produced by the compass actuates an electric or hydraulic motor which extends or retracts a rod or hydraulic cylinder, moving the rudder so as to bring the boat back on course. The compass carries out a desired/actual value comparison and continues the steering operation until the vessel is back on the desired course. There is a direct relationship between

- The steering force
- The speed with which the steering force is exerted
- The current consumption

The physical constants between these factors are fixed, so the only relationship that matters on a sailing yacht – steering performance (output)/current consumption (input) – is always a compromise. It is never possible to obtain maximum steering performance using minimum power.

This gives rise to a dilemma, since an electric motor can be geared to produce either a lot of power slowly or a little power quickly (this relates to a car managing a steep gradient slowly in first gear, but not at all in top gear).

Autopilots are distinguished by motor capacity. This automatically fixes the relationship between the force applied by the push rod and its speed of operation. Virtually all autopilot manufacturers rely on this proven arrangement, and systems with variable speed motor drives are very seldom seen. Such pronounced gearing-down of the force from the electric motor (to produce more force at the push rod) is not practical anyway, since the corrective movement of the rudder would then be effected too slowly to bring the vessel efficiently back to the desired course.

To identify the appropriate autopilot it is necessary first to determine the maximum rudder torque for the boat in question; the critical factors here are rudder size (length and width), counterbalance (distance from the centre of the rudder post to the leading edge of the rudder) and speed potential of the boat. The rudder torque can either be calculated or worked out empirically, that is by actually measuring the force on the tiller or wheel. If the maximum load on the rudder exceeds the maximum torque of the drive unit, failure is inevitable. Choose a low power consumption model for a relatively heavy boat, and the steering performance will be less than wonderful. Choose a system which will be constantly at its limits and it will need replacing long before an overdimensioned one. Choose a powerful autopilot, and no battery in the world will be able to meet the power demand without regular recharging. Every compromise has its price!

Cockpit autopilots for tiller steering

Push rod systems, in which an electric motor is connected via a transmission directly to a push rod, are the most straightforward form of autopilot. The push rod is extended or retracted to move the tiller.

Simple cockpit autopilots consist of a single module which includes the compass, the motor and the push rod. In larger cockpit models, the control unit and compass are separate modules which may be linked to other external transducers via a data bus. Autohelm indicates its network-compatible instruments with the 'ST' (SeaTalk) prefix and Navico uses the 'CORUS' badge.

Tiller push rod systems are not particularly powerful, and are therefore only suitable for smaller boats. They use relatively small (power-saving) electric motors whose force has to be multiplied by major gearing down before it is applied to the push rod. This makes them noisy and the

sound of a cockpit autopilot in operation is quite intrusive. Cockpit autopilots are relatively frugal in normal operation but, under high loads, consumption can approach 3 amps. They tend to be rather ponderous in their movements. The following systems are available:

Autohelm 800
Autohelm ST 1000
Autohelm ST 2000
Autohelm ST 4000 Tiller
Navico TP 100
Navico TP 300 CX

Cockpit autopilots for wheel steering

Wheel steering autopilot systems are similar to those described above, except that the course corrections are effected by a driving belt, toothed belt or toothed wheel acting on a pulley attached to the vessel's wheel. Cockpit autopilots for wheel steering may be linked to a data network. The following systems are available:

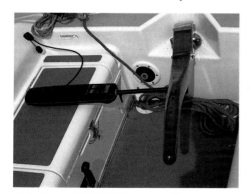

Autohelm ST 800 tiller autopilot.

Navico WP 300 CX wheel autopilot.

Autohelm ST 3000
Autohelm ST 4000 Wheel
Navico WP 100
Navico WP 300 CX

Inboard autopilots

Inboard autopilots use push rod or hydraulic systems with powerful motors which are connected to the rudder post or quadrant and turn the main rudder directly. It is also possible to replace the mechanical linkage and shaft with a hydraulic system in which a hydraulic pump provides oil pressure to drive a hydraulic cylinder which in turn moves the main rudder. This type of system is suitable for larger boats. Vessels over 21 m/60 ft in length with sizeable hydraulic rudder arrangements use constantly running pumps controlled by solenoid valves for the autopilot.

The three modules of an inboard autopilot

Control unit

The control unit is used to call up all the functions of the autopilot and any other modules linked via the data bus. It is usually operated via push buttons (Autohelm) or turning knobs (Robertson). Display sizes vary and, not surprisingly, larger displays are generally easier to read. Modern high-contrast LCD displays will fade if exposed to excessive direct sunlight, so they should ideally be mounted vertically and never flat on the deck. It is usually possible to fit additional control units wherever they are needed, so the operator is not restricted to the main cockpit. A hand-held remote control unit provides even more freedom to move about the deck. Joysticks offering direct control of the autopilot drive unit are also available.

Central processing unit

The central processing unit consists of: course computer, compass, rudder position indicator, windvane transducer, and peripherals.

Course computer

The course computer, installed below deck, is responsible for processing all commands and signals, for calculating the rudder movements necessary for course correction and for actuating the drive unit. In short, it links software and hardware and converts signals into actions. There are two kinds of course computer:

• The manual version which is adjusted and set up by the user and/or installer;
• The auto-adaptive version which learns from recent operations and from recorded data.

Both have their advantages, but sailors may well prefer the ease of the auto-adaptive black box. Aside from seeing to a few basic decisions (mode of gain, auto tack, compass or windvane), the user has only to sit back and watch that the software carries on doing its job. The overriding aim is to combine high performance with reduced power consumption and neither option is perfect: factory programmed units are never properly set up for real conditions, and manually-adjusted units are also unlikely to deliver their full potential unless the user is a professional.

Compass

Compasses work best on land. Once afloat, the trouble starts: pitching,

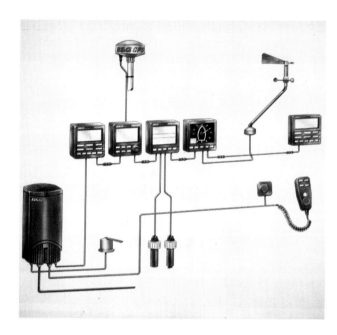

The modules of an inboard pilot; a Brookes & Gatehouse example.

rolling, heeling, acceleration and deceleration all make things difficult for a compass. The course computer needs a clear, readable signal from the compass to control the drive properly – an autopilot course can only be as good as the steering impulse from the compass.

The position of the compass is very important. Consider the following points prior to installation:

• The further the compass is from the boat's centre, the greater the number of movements which will have to be filtered out.
• Any variations in local magnetic fields will prevent an accurate signal. The compass should be kept well away from electric motors, pumps, generators, radios, TVs, navigation instruments, power cables and metal objects.
• Compasses prefer constant temperatures; avoid sites exposed to sunlight or heat from the engine, cooker or heater.

Below deck near the base of the mast is a good spot on most cruising designs, provided they do not have a steel hull. The most stable point on more extreme modern yachts is further aft, normally about one third of the way from the stern to the bow. On steel boats there are different ways to get proper steering signals. An arrangement in which a magnetic compass with course detector is fitted under the compass bowl detects changes in magnetic fields and has been used most successfully by Robertson on commercial fishing vessels. Other manufacturers position their fluxgate compasses above deck or even in the mast, not always the ideal location because of its accentuated motion. Careful installation and thorough calibration of the compass are particularly important on steel boats (a fluxgate compass cannot be used below deck on a steel boat).

The distance from the compass to the course computer should be kept as short as possible to minimise the problem of voltage drops. The longer this distance, the thicker the cables that will be needed. One final point to bear in mind regarding installation: the compass should ideally be easily accessible in its final position.

There are three types of compass to choose from, the magnetic compass, the fluxgate compass and the gyrocompass. Fluxgate sensors which supply the course computer with electronic course data are standard with nearly all manufacturers. Steering performance in testing conditions can be optimised by installing a special fluxgate system. Autohelm uses a 'GyroPlus' transducer while Robertson has a novel type of compass in which fluxgate signals are translated into frequency signals whose variations can more easily be monitored. Further optimisation measures include fluid damping and electronic averaging. The quality of the final signal for actual steering actions is directly related to the price and quality of the sensor unit. You really do get what you pay for, and unfortunately the price range, which starts at around £200 for an ordinary fluxgate compass and £240 for a magnetic compass and course detector, extends all the way up to £9000 for a high-tech gyrocompass unit.

Rudder position indicator
The rudder position transducer is arranged on the rudder and informs the course computer of the position of the rudder. It can be fitted inside the drive unit (protected from errant footsteps) or externally at the rudder post (more vulnerable).

Windvane transducer
A transducer attached to a windvane or to the masthead passes informa-tion on the apparent wind angle to the course computer.

Peripherals
Signals from other navigation equipment such as Decca, GPS, Loran, radar, log and depth sounder can also be fed to the course computer to give additional data to aid precise steering.

Drive unit

There are four alternatives:

1 Mechanical linear drive unit
An electric motor operates the push rod mechanically via a transmission. These drives are similar in principle to cockpit autopilots, but are considerably more powerful. The electric motor can be constant speed (simple and cheap but power-hungry) or variable speed (more efficient). The mechanical linear drive is more energy efficient than its hydraulic linear sister but is also more susceptible to mechanical overload under extreme conditions. Wear and tear on this kind of mechanical drive also increase the operating noise of the unit under load, so it will get louder

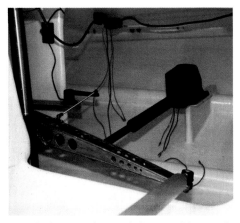

Autohelm mechanical linear drive unit aboard the 18 m/60 ft ULDB *Budapest.*

as it gets older and could eventually become irritating. Depending on the particular use and the size of the system it may be advisable to use metal for the transmission components since plastic is not always able to withstand the heavy loading associated with extended operation. Autohelm offers the 'Grand Prix' package as an upgrade for its linear drive units; Robertson and almost all other manufacturers fit metal transmission components as standard.

A hydraulic linear drive unit needs more installation space than a simple mechanical linear unit to accommodate the balancing ram which protrudes from the back. Mark Parkin of Simrad UK has observed that quite a number of naval architects 'forget about the bigger space required by hydraulic rams' and so end up having to fit a linear drive.

2 Hydraulic linear drive unit
The push rod is operated by a hydraulic pump. Hydraulic linear drives appear on large yachts with particularly high rudder forces. The drives may be supplied either by separately installed hydraulic pumps (Autohelm, VDO) or by pumps directly incorporated into the push rod system (Brookes & Gatehouse, Robertson). Robertson also offers 'dual drives', in which two linear drives double the force applied. Hydraulic drives are protected against mechanical overload by an overload valve, which opens above a certain oil pressure, and by the inherent 'oil cushion'. A hydraulic linear drive produces far less operating noise than a mechanical linear drive and will remain smoother and quieter, and hence more pleasant to have aboard, throughout its life. Hydraulic

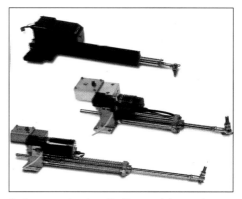

Robertson hydraulic linear drive units.

linear drives also last much longer, an important advantage for long distance cruising, and only a replacement set of seals need be carried as spares. As mentioned, hydraulic linear drives have a balancing ram which protrudes from the back of the unit. They therefore need to be mounted higher up to prevent the balancing ram striking the inside of the hull.

3 Hydraulic drive units
These electromechanical hydraulic pumps tap directly into the existing wheel steering hydraulic system. A constantly running pump may be used to supply the force required to steer boats of 25 tonnes or more. The constantly high pressure introduces sudden high loads into the steering system with every rudder movement, and the resulting noise has earned this type of drive the name 'bang-bang pilot'.

4 Chain drive unit
An electric motor operates the main rudder via a chain. Chain drives are preferred where space is limited or where the rod-operated or geared wheel steering on an older boat precludes the use of other drive units.

Blue Papillon, a 29 m/95 ft Jongert steered by a Segatron autopilot.

Whitlock steering wheel drives offer the option of an installed mechanical motor which taps into the system's transmission below deck. Only the cpu and control module then remain to be fitted.

The drive unit has to be connected to the rudder with a comparatively short arm either via its own small tiller or at the quadrant itself. Both alternatives demand very strong mounting on the side of the hull, and structural reinforcements will often be required.

The existing wheel steering should be mechanically disconnected when the autopilot is in use to reduce inertia. This can be done using:

a) A mechanical pin clutch (Edson),
b) A mechanical pin lock (Alpha),
c) A solenoid activated mechanical clutch (Autohelm), or
d) A solenoid activated hydraulic bypass.

If the manual steering arrangement is not properly disconnected, the autopilot will operate with a delay and consume more power. Equally, when the boat is being steered manually the drive unit should be disconnected or bypassed to afford better sensitivity on the helm and to allow the full range of rudder angle, which is normally limited under autopilot. Reducing inertia for manual helming also means less work for the hand on the wheel.

When mechanically disconnected, the drive unit connecting arm should be fixed in position to prevent it from bouncing around. The end stops of the drive unit must be within the maximum limits of the rudder itself to prevent the autopilot from driving the hydraulic ram into the rudder stops.

It is absolutely essential that every autopilot has an emergency stop switch within easy reach of the helm in case the system runs into difficulties or manual steering suddenly becomes necessary. This switch should never be below deck. The distance from the helm to the nav-station or circuit breaker panel is simply too great in an emergency where the delay could result in damage to the autopilot or worse. Robertson autopilots all have such a switch included in every deck display unit.

It is extremely unwise to attempt DIY installation of an inboard autopilot. The procedure is very complex and there are far too many potential errors for the inexperienced yacht owner to make. Robertson, for one, refuses outright to provide any warranty for DIY systems.

Integrated systems

Until a few years ago it was generally the case that boat owners acquired their instruments one by one: depth sounder, radar, compass, wind instrument, Decca, GPS, plotter, boat speed indicator and autopilot might easily be individually installed stand-alone units from several different manufacturers.

The situation today is very different, with a few major suppliers offering complete systems from which the sailor can choose as few or as many instruments as desired. Essential to this advance was the development of a specialised data bus and data transfer protocol: functions such as the steering performance of an autopilot module can now be optimised in more demanding systems by connecting a dedicated course computer. An autopilot steering a boat between two waypoints obtained from a GPS interface can thus correct for cross-track

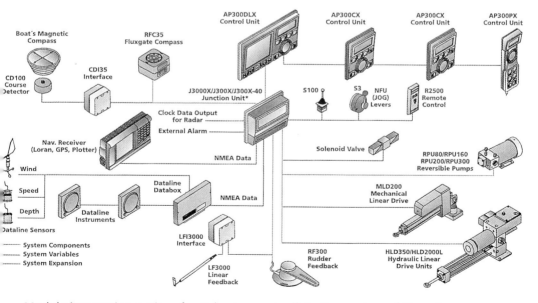

Module integration options for Robertson autopilots. By courtesy of Simrad.

error caused by currents running perpendicular to the boat's course.

The changing role of companies within the industry from instrument manufacturers to system suppliers explains the current extreme concentration of the market on just a few major players.

Autopilots may be divided into three groups:

1 Stand-alone systems that operate solely on the basis of a windvane or compass signal (eg Autohelm 800);
2 Systems that are linked to other modules via a data bus (eg Sea-Talk from Autohelm, Robnet by Robertson) and/or an NMEA 0183 interface;
3 Systems in which the individual modules are linked exclusively by the manufacturer's own data bus (B & G).

Today, most autopilots operate as one module within a complex system. NMEA (National Marine Electronics Association) interfaces offer the prospect of expanding such a system to include instruments from other manufacturers. The claim that instruments from different system suppliers could communicate with each other using the same interfaces seemed rather optimistic at one time. There were, as many sailors discovered to their cost, several standards in existence even for NMEA interfaces, and of course no instrument manufacturer was to blame for any incompatibility; serious communication problems are always the fault of the instrument on the other side of the interface! These problems have now for the most part been resolved. Company-specific data buses do still tend to work much faster than NMEA interfaces, however, and the importance of speed cannot be exaggerated. The delay in the transmission of a steering impulse from one sensor unit to another can never be too short.

Provided with a fluxgate compass/gyrocompass signal optimised by integrated navigation modules, an autopilot is perfectly capable of steering a boat from waypoint to waypoint – assuming, of course, that the wind decides to co-operate.

Navigating down below with the Autohelm Navplotter 100.

The windvane transducer

Almost all autopilots can be linked to a windvane transducer. This enables them to take the apparent wind angle signal as steering impulse. The signal comes either from the masthead unit or from a small windvane at the stern. Neither alternative produces particularly satisfactory results in any kind of swell, since the movements of the masthead unit caused by the motion of the boat, the effects of upwash from the mainsail or the confused readings of the stern-mounted unit caused by disturbed air have to be considerably damped and processed to obtain a useful signal. The small size of autopilot windvanes often contributes to such problems.

The volume of data required to produce precise and practicable course commands for the steering module when using the course computer to calculate the apparent wind angle is substantial: rolling, pitching, speed, acceleration, wind angle and possibly also true parameters (true wind angle etc) must all be processed. When sailing, the autopilot should always be set to steer to either the windvane transducer or the compass signal, and never to a navigation instrument or waypoint. The importance of sailing to the apparent wind angle cannot be understated; ignore it and the boat loses all its drive.

Power consumption

The power consumption of an autopilot is determined not only by the rating of the model chosen but also by the following factors:

- Length and displacement of the vessel: The more boat there is to move, the greater the power consumption.
- Type of rudder: A keel-mounted rudder requires more force because it is impossible to balance. A rudder on a skeg can have a balance portion below the skeg and is therefore easier to steer. A fully balanced spade rudder without a skeg is lightest on the helm.
- Speed with which corrective rudder movements must be made: This depends on how well the boat holds a course, and is therefore also influenced by its shape below the waterline.
- Sail trim, weather helm: Poorly trimmed sails and continuous weather helm are always more of a drain on the autopilot than a well-balanced boat.
- Sea conditions: Bigger seas and increased yawing require more frequent steering interventions by the autopilot.
- Desired steering precision: The more exactly the course must be held, the greater the amount of work there is for the autopilot.
- Software/manual adjustment: The more refined the course computer algorithms, ie the better suited they are to the particular boat they are steering, the lower the power consumption will be. The power consumption of a manually adjustable unit depends to a considerable extent on the sensitivity of the controls and on how easy it is to set them up properly.

Conserving power

Optimising the vessel with respect to the above points can considerably reduce average power consumption. Once this has been done, the only remaining measure is to reduce the frequency of course corrections. This amounts in practice to increasing the angle by which the boat may deviate from the set course before the autopilot responds in other words, this allowing the boat a greater range of movement between active steering interventions.

All modern autopilots are auto-adaptive, that is they are programmed to recognise certain regular patterns of yawing. This helps them shorten their operating cycle and reduce the length of time for which the motor is running. It also enables them promptly to correct the course early on in a recurrent motion, so avoiding more vigorous rudder movements later on. Unfortunately we have now reached the end of the list of power-saving measures.

The manufacturers base their average power consumption figures for cockpit autopilots on a 25 per cent operating cycle. This assumes in terms of actual autopilot running time that, per hour, the boat is actively steered for 15 minutes and holds itself on course with no action at all from the helm for the other 45 minutes. These figures may seem just a little optimistic; actual power consumption, therefore, will often be higher.

Fitting out for an extended voyage really brings home the gulf between the theory and practice of power consumption. Energy management is essential here since all the power consumed on board must first be generated on board. The difference between the manufacturers' rated average power consumption and the actual autopilot motor running time can be enormous; real situations are never 'average' and the actual power consumption is always higher.

A boat equipped with just a depth sounder, a handheld GPS, paraffin cabin lights, a windvane steering system and without an ice box – that is to say, a vessel whose power consumption is reduced to the minimum – will hardly ever run its batteries close to exhaustion. This boat does not, however, bear much resemblance to the average passage yacht. The ARC fleet that passes through the Canaries every autumn shows a clear trend: in the last ten years alone, the average length of participating yachts has grown to around 13 m/44 ft, while the number of sub-33-footers has dwindled to barely a handful. The boats are generally equipped to a very high standard as well, with most carrying navigation instruments such as GPS, plotters and radar, short wave, SSB and VHF radios, refrigerator, pumps, water maker and interior and exterior lights.

Combining the 24-hour average power consumption of each of these appliances for a 13 m/44 ft boat in warmer latitudes gives a total of 120 ampere-hours (Ah) – even without an electric autopilot running. This example clearly illustrates the care needed in budgeting for energy aboard a sailing yacht. The impact of an autopilot on this energy budget is very substantial, particularly if the system has been chosen for its high performance rather than low power consumption. There are books devoted solely to the subject of energy management on board: pay too little heed to this complex issue before you cast off and you can count on a nasty reminder somewhere out at sea.

The manufacturer's recommended autopilot for our exemplary 13 m/44 ft boat draws between 2.7 and 6 A per hour, which means that if run

Navigating on deck with Autohelm.

continuously it will push up the vessel's total power consumption by at least another 50 per cent over a 24-hour period. We should also bear in mind here that some units in the vessel's electrical system will fail if the voltage falls below 10.5 V. Against this background, a seemingly large battery capacity of 600 Ah begins to look less impressive.

Wind, water, wave and solar generators can help, but even these (depending on the conditions) are no guarantee against a few hours of enforced motoring every day (as well-known circumnavigator and race organiser Jimmy Cornell confirmed after debriefing skippers at the end of his Europa 92 race). Whenever one of the additional generators malfunctions or fails, increased engine running time inevitably results. Without good sound-proofing, the iron sail can rapidly become an unwelcome intrusion into life aboard. The extra heat from the engine is often a bonus as well, just right to ease the afternoon chill in Bermuda...

Energy matters are of course less critical on boats used mainly for weekends and holidays, since this kind of sailing normally involves plenty of motoring and shore power is always at hand for recharging.

Range of adjustment of an autopilot: Autohelm 6000/7000

1 *The rudder gain*, which has nine settings, specifies how much the rudder should be moved to return the boat to a desired course. Oversteering will result if the angle is set too high; understeering will result if it is set too low.

2 *The rudder damping function* has nine positions and serves to damp yawing motions.

3 *The rudder amidships position* in the rudder reference transducer has an adjustment range of $-7°$ to $+7°$.

4 *The rudder limit function* prevents the autopilot reaching maximum lock at full power, which could cause mechanical damage.

5 *Boat turn rate* determines how quickly the boat will turn when the autopilot makes course corrections.

6 The autopilot can be set for an *average cruise speed* of anywhere between 4 and 60 knots (sailing boat or powerboat).

7 *The adjustable off-course alarm* sounds when the vessel's course deviates from the desired course by more than a set maximum (in degrees) for longer than 20 seconds.

8 *There are four trim settings.* This function controls the additional rudder movement necessary to counter off-centre thrust (eg when operating a propeller mounted to one side, only used when motoring).

9 *The Joystick* has two settings, but these are not particularly relevant for sailing boats.

10 The control unit can be set for *linear* or *hydraulic drive*.

11 *The response angle function* has nine positions. It ensures that the response of the autopilot is appropriately delayed if there is slack or play in the steering system.

12 *Compass deviation* taken from a chart can be input.

13 *The adjustable northerly/southerly turning error compensation feature* is used in areas where the orien-

tation of North is uncertain to ensure that the compass receives an accurate signal.

14 There are three settings for the *reaction speed* of the autopilot; the higher the value set, the greater the steering precision and, consequently, the power consumption.

All the functions mentioned are initially set at the factory. Each one can be adjusted on board, though, and it is essential that they are individually matched to the characteristics of the vessel.

To summarise, each model of autopilot gives a certain level of steering performance that is dictated by its range of technical features and that cannot be improved. All that is left once the autopilot is correctly set up is to increase the time between steering corrections, and hence save power, by ensuring that the boat is balanced and the sails are properly trimmed. It should be obvious that selecting a greater degree of steering accuracy will lead to more frequent rudder movements and increased power consumption.

The limits of autopilots

Even the very best autopilots struggle when beating into a shifting wind. This is because they do not detect small changes in wind direction (the sails back). The only solution is to set a lower course which, unfortunately, means losing distance to windward. It is possible to connect a windvane to the course computer but, as we discussed above, this does not always produce satisfactory results.

Blue water sailing, though, means winds from astern. The passage routes around the world are universally known; every long-distance sailor heads straight for the all but infallible trades, dreaming of pleasant sailing before the wind. It is therefore imperative that autopilots, and indeed any type of self-steering, can hold an off-the-wind course. No experienced sailor expects miracles of the autopilot: a steering accuracy of 5° in the trades with a big following sea is just not realistic. Equally, it is no good if your autopilot follows the general course with occasional 100° excursions – you may still arrive, but probably not where you intended.

The only way to be sure of good steering from an unassisted autopilot is to buy a fast and powerful system. While nothing else will be able to guarantee adequate steering performance in all wind and sea conditions, this solution does inevitably lead us back again to questions of power consumption. Ultimately each skipper has to decide, in the light of energy budgets and daily power requirements, which answer best suits his or her particular needs.

Issues of power consumption often tempt a skipper to risk a slightly undersized autopilot. There is no avoiding the loss of performance such a system will suffer as conditions deteriorate. With no reserves of speed or power to meet the increased demands it will eventually be overwhelmed, reacting too slowly and with too little force to keep the boat on course. Mechanical overload is likewise a threat in such circumstances. Chuck Hawley of West Marine, one of the world's largest autopilot dealers with its own service centres and more than 400 outlets in the USA goes even further, stating in the company's very comprehensive catalogue that a cockpit autopilot 'will need repairs' on a longer trip. He continues *'we do not recommend that you use a cockpit autopilot for long distance sailing unless one of the following applies:*

1 You have a back-up autopilot in case the first one fails
2 You have a wind vane and are not dependent solely on the autopilot
3 You love steering by hand for long hours.'

The rated operating speeds and drive unit thrusts of the various cockpit autopilot systems are a good indicator of the steering performance you can expect.

Electromagnetic interference

Electromagnetic interference originating from onboard high-frequency transmitters and receivers was once a common problem, causing autopilots to make sudden anomalous course changes. The European CE (Electromagnetic Compatibility) Standard should prevent this kind of disruption of the autopilot in the future. Existing electronics systems can best be protected by ensuring that all power cables are well insulated.

Extreme sailing

Autopilots are unable to steer in areas where North is uncertain. Ocean sailors in races like the BOC and Vendée Globe run into problems in the high latitudes of the South Pacific with the autopilot suddenly cutting out after losing its fix on North. Nandor Fa, skipper of the Hungarian yacht *K & H Bank* in the 1992 Vendée Globe (singlehanded, non-stop race around the world),

received the following answer from the manufacturer of his Robertson system after faxing for help with his confused autopilot: 'Please perform three complete circles in calm water within a few minutes – this will enable the compass to reorient itself'. Given the chaotic sea conditions in the Southern Oceans, this was not the most practical piece of advice. Only after several days of steering by hand did Fa hit upon the idea of removing the compass and rotating it as gently as possible in his hand. Since then he has used Autohelm systems, which now have special GPS-supported software to help the compass maintain clear steering signals even when North is uncertain. The close collaboration between manufacturers and ocean sailors in events like the BOC and Vendée Globe ensures continued development of the systems. Virtually all the boats in these races are now steered by Autohelm.

Nandor Fa on board *K & H Bank*.

One result of this collaboration has been the development of stronger drive components for blue water use. Autohelm introduced the 'Grand-Prix' upgrade package for its 4000/6000/7000 series in 1996. The standard Delrin (plastic) load-bearing components in the drive are replaced with bronze equivalents. Plastic, as several long-distance skippers have had the misfortune to discover, sometimes fails to measure up to the high stresses placed on drive components. However, for holidays and daysailing, when extreme loads are rare, plastic components are perfectly adequate. Hydraulic systems are immune to overloading problems of this nature as they have no mechanical drive components (Autohelm 6000/7000 with hydraulic or hydraulic linear drive, B & G Network, Hydra 2, Robertson, VDO, Cetrek, Navico, Coursemaster, Silva, Alpha, W – H).

Autopilots for different purposes

Holiday and weekend sailing

Most sailors use their boats primarily at the weekend or for holidays, which partially explains the rapid spread of electric autopilots. Power consumption is not really an issue on one-day trips, and the quality of steering performance is also relatively unimportant since it is always possible to steer by hand if necessary. Sea conditions rarely impair steering quality as the majority of weekend sailors do not venture into exposed waters. Taking the helm in any case forms part of the fun for the average sailor, so the autopilot is really just a convenience. It sees to the tedious work (steering while under engine) and gives the crew the freedom to eat together, for example. Autopilots, at least the cockpit models, are also within the financial reach of the average sailor.

The significance of a yacht's autopilot grows with the length of the voyage. There will generally be no problem finding volunteers to steer on a shorter trip, but on a longer trip manual steering becomes tedious and the autopilot will eventually be called into action.

Autohelm has devoted far more effort to the weekend and holiday sector than any other manufacturer and is the world-wide market leader; thanks in particular to its cockpit-mounted range, the company has captured around 90 per cent of the market.

Coastal sailing

Coastal sailing in unprotected waters normally involves longer voyages. A small crew soon tires of steering and it is here that the steering quality of the autopilot starts to matter. Sea state and factors such as tidal streams, shallows, narrow channels and winds from forward of the beam all impair the performance of autopilots. Rough seas make life difficult for them, and as the waves increase in height and frequency the limits of a particular system quickly become apparent. Not surprisingly, intelligent and adaptive systems cope better with trying conditions than factory-set units that cannot be adjusted.

The general standard of equipment in this type of sailing is very high. The importance of good steering performance means that powerful inboard pilots connected directly to the main rudder are much more common;

underpowered systems are soon exposed on the open sea. Although more powerful autopilots are inevitably hungrier, this rarely leads to battery problems since coastal sailing includes fairly regular motoring.

Blue water sailing

An autopilot stands or falls on its blue water performance. An underpowered system on the ocean reacts too slowly, too weakly and with too much delay to keep the boat on course, with increased yawing being the result. The fear of losing steerage, of rounding up into the wind or worse, and damaging the rig or boat, gives every sailor nightmares. If your autopilot is untrustworthy in a sea you could find yourself at the helm for a very long time.

The choice of autopilot becomes a survival issue for short-, double- or singlehanded sailing: a thousand miles at sea is more than enough to reveal the gulf between theory and reality, and choosing the wrong system could jeopardise the whole voyage. This is evidenced by the large number of would-be passage sailors who, reminded of the enormous importance of good self-steering on the initial leg of their voyage, stop off at Vilamoura, Gibraltar or Las Palmas to fit back-up systems, buy spare parts or add a windvane gear to supplement their autopilot. It is no coincidence that companies like Hydrovane and Windpilot deliver so many of their windvane steering systems to these strategic European jumping-off points!

Although autopilots are standard on blue water yachts, the limitations of the different models (underpowered system, mechanical failures) dictate that they do not in fact steer continuously. A certain amount of manual steering is therefore unavoidable, something that is not always pleasant for the person on watch and that disrupts life aboard. The performance of electric autopilots drops sharply as wind and waves increase, so heavy weather steering often falls to a human helm as well. He or she, of course, has the advantage of being able to see (and hopefully avoid!) breaking waves.

Jimmy Cornell, organiser of races for long-distance recreational sailors, established in his debriefing after the Europa 92 round the world race that automatic systems steered for only 50 per cent of the total time at sea. Manual steering was preferred the rest of the time, either to improve speed and carry more sail area or because self-steering systems were just not able to cope with the conditions. Some crews simply did not trust their technology. Almost all the skippers used the autopilot when motoring through calms even if they chose to steer by hand when there was enough wind to sail.

The combination of off-the-wind sailing and long following seas characteristic of blue water passage making sets the stiffest challenge to any autopilot. The need for quick and forceful corrective rudder movements drives up the pilot's power consumption and saps away at the vessel's energy budget. This once again highlights the fundamental importance of responsible energy planning for any vessel intending to rely solely on an autopilot. The average power consumption of the autopilots used in the Europa 92 race was approximately 4.9 Ah (average boat length 15–18 m / 42–50 ft).

We must add at this juncture that the electromechanical reliability of autopilot systems still leaves something to be desired, particularly under the conditions likely in blue water sailing. This means in practical terms that sooner or later almost every autopilot is going to fail completely and manual steering will be unavoidable. The American Seven Seas Cruising Association (SSCA) reported following a recent owner survey that the average autopilot serves for about 300 hours before failing. A major study in America found that autopilots normally have a useful life of about five years before they have to be replaced. This means that in the US alone thousands of units expire every year, a sobering thought even though the survey does include sail, power and fishing boats. The prospective blue water sailor should find one look at the list in the Las Palmas ARC office of the skippers requesting autopilot repairs enough to trigger deep concern.

Not surprisingly, bigger electric circuits with a larger number of components are more susceptible to gremlins, and the failure of a single, tiny component can be enough in some cases to cripple a whole system. Moisture is another challenge: conditions aboard are always damp, even below deck, and some units are not as waterproof as they could be. Overheating can lead to problems as well. Autohelm's choice of black for its cockpit autopilots is particularly problematic in tropical climes since the colour causes thermally induced operating temperatures to rise to the point where faults can occur. The sailor's only remedy here is a tin of white paint!

It is striking that those who live aboard their boats tend to revert in the end to the most basic level of equipment, dispensing with any unnecessary gear and reducing clutter aboard; that a good self-steering system still merits a place underlines its importance. One-time pharmacist Lorenz Findeisen has been roving the Caribbean with his Westerly 39 for years. His answer to the question of how his level of equipment has evolved was as follows: 'Most of it broke a long time ago, but I'm not really bothered. As long as the anchor tackle, cooker and my windvane gear keep going I can carry on sailing.'

Autohelm is the market leader for inboard autopilots. Robertson has considerable experience as a system supplier for merchant vessels and is probably in second place. B & G, which concentrates mainly on precision transducers for racing boats, supplies quite a few of its Network and Hydra 2 systems to boats in this sector.

Racing

For our purposes, races fall into two categories:

1 Fully crewed boats

These are nearly always steered by hand. This applies in all races, from round-the-buoys to the most famous of all, the Whitbread Round the World Race. Whitbread boats and others for the same kind of racing are extreme in all respects: extreme in their ultralight construction (ultralight displacement boats or ULDBs) which allows them to surf at great speed; extreme in their rigs, which are oversized and infinitely tweakable; and extreme in their aim of constantly maintaining absolute maximum speed. Extreme racing is an

Racing with a large crew.

Start of the Vendée Globe in November 1992.

exhausting sport which pushes crews to the limit and often, in the biggest races where expectant sponsors demand success and publicity, beyond their limits. When autopilots are used on boats of this nature (on delivery passages, for example), only computerised systems with 'intelligent' steering measure up (eg B & G Hydra/Hercules, Autohelm 6000/ 7000, Robertson AP 300 X or similar).

2 ULDBs in singlehanded races

Competitors in the Vendée Globe, the singlehanded non-stop sprint around the world which starts from Les Sables d'Olonne in France every four years, rely exclusively on electric autopilots. The race, which includes 50- and 60-foot classes, is viewed by autopilot manufacturers as the ultimate test; the harshest conditions are guaranteed and the use of windvane

steering systems is virtually out of the question (see Ocean racing, p 80). Some older, slower vessels in the BOC Race (singlehanded around the world in stages) carry windvane steering systems as their back-up, but here too autopilots do most of the steering.

ULDBs, which rarely have any kind of engine, rely on generators, solar cells or wind generators to maintain the power supply. The boats can reach speeds of 25 knots, so only the most powerful, 'intelligent' computerised systems are strong and fast enough to keep them on course. Autopilots are installed on every boat and steer most of the time. Although competitors in the long singlehanded races tend to follow a ten-minute waking/sleeping cycle, they never for one moment stop thinking about safety and boat speed. Nandor Fa lost about 12 kg/26 lb in one Vendée

The 18.2 m/60 ft ULDB *Charente Maritime*, fitted with a Windpilot Pacific, took part in the1988 Vendée Globe .

Globe and knows only too well how the effects of this kind of deprivation endure.

Autohelm is a very big presence on the extreme sailing scene. The company has devoted particular attention to this area and has earned its success by maintaining a continuous presence before, during and after races, by making considerable service efforts, and by cultivating its close relationship with the participants.

Choosing an autopilot

Cockpit autopilots lose effectiveness rather quickly as the size of vessel increases. The manufacturers specify their most powerful models for boats no heavier than 9 tonnes and even this can seem optimistic in more taxing operating conditions. Cockpit autopilots also become relatively power-hungry at higher loads and it is therefore unwise to select a unit for which the boat in question represents the very limit of the rated operating range.

The chief decision with regard to inboard autopilots is the type of drive unit to install. The choice between mechanical linear, hydraulic linear and hydraulic drives depends essentially on:

• Boat size
• Existing main rudder steering arrangement
• Capacity of batteries
• Intended use

Although mechanical linear drives draw less current and are often more convenient for smaller boats, they tend to lack sufficient power for boats of 12 m/40 ft or more. Hydraulic linear drives are better for bigger boats with their higher rudder loads and larger battery banks. Hydraulic drives are well suited to boats with hydraulic main steering, and a continuously running hydraulic pump is the best option for maxis and bigger.

The autopilot operating speed necessary to keep a particular boat on track has to be calculated. Long keel, long distance cruising boats can manage with a powerful but more slowly operating system; about 5–6° of rudder movement per second (no load) will generally suffice. A light-built 30 footer with a fin keel and a balanced rudder will need something like 15–20° (no load) but the force applied at the rudder will never have to be very high.

Yacht owners will normally require the manufacturer's help to calculate the specific needs of their particular boat. A high level of support and service from a manufacturer at this point bodes well and will inevitably help to win over an owner. For powerboaters, who rarely take their vessels beyond the reach of service mechanics, the consequences of an error of judgement at the decision stage are frustration and annoyance. For a blue water sailor they can be disastrous: days on end at the helm with no relief.

A final consideration when choosing an autopilot, and one which you ignore at your peril, is comfort below deck. A noisy drive unit can make an otherwise desirable cabin almost uninhabitable.

· 4 ·

Windvane steering systems

Windvane steering systems obtain their steering impulse from the apparent wind angle. The advantage of this is that a sailing boat likewise generates its drive from its position relative to the apparent wind. Once the sails and windvane have been set at the appropriate angle to the wind, the boat will continue to steer this angle indefinitely and the sails will always be properly trimmed.

Wind direction is the key consideration when planning any voyage. If the wind blows from astern it is possible to set the rhumb-line course and enjoy a comfortable trip from A to B via the shortest route. When the wind is on the nose, however, tacking is unavoidable and a compass course is useless; the direct route is not the quickest if the sails are backing.

The three elements of a windvane steering system are the windvane, the linkage and the rudder. We cover each in turn below:

The windvane

The steering impulse in a windvane gear comes from the windvane. The vane takes its energy from the apparent wind flowing across its surface at the angle set. There are two types of vane, the horizontal vane and the vertical vane.

The vertical vane

How it works

The vertical or V vane rotates about a vertical axis (the same principle as a weathervane), see Fig 4.1a. It always points directly into the wind, so the effective windvane area (the area actually subject to the action of the wind) is never very big. When the boat strays off course the windvane is deflected by no more than the amount in degrees of the deviation. The steering impulse generated by this deflection can only deliver a limited amount of force since a V vane generates little torque.

Adjustment

Adjusting a V vane to the wind direction could hardly be easier: when free to rotate, it always points exactly into the wind and requires no special setting. It can be adjusted for different wind strengths just by moving it in or out along its mounting bracket. Increasing the distance between the vane and its shaft (longer lever) gives increased power for light airs. Reducing the distance (shorter lever) helps to reduce vibrations in the vane gear in heavier airs when power is not a problem.

Shape

Air flow across a vertical windvane is always laminar, so aerodynamic

Fig 4.1a V vane

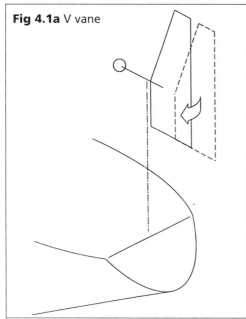

V vane, Windpilot Atlantik auxiliary rudder system.

sections or wedge-shaped designs with flow separation edges are the most efficient shapes. Not only are both alternatives heavy, but they are also complex and expensive to build, so almost all manufacturers prefer simple flat designs.

Area

V vanes need to be quite large in area (up to $1 \text{ m}^2/10\frac{1}{2} \text{ ft}^2$) to enable them to deliver satisfactory steering impulses as well as the necessary steering force. They take up a quite alot of space on the transom owing to their size and turning circle, so permanent backstays, mizzen masts and davits can easily get in the way.

Counterweight

Because of its substantial size and weight, a V vane should be perfectly balanced by a counterweight. This is particularly important in the light air position for otherwise steering impulses can be generated by the

Wedge-profile V vane, Saye's Rig.

heel of the boat. It is less critical in the heavy air position when the vane is up against its shaft because the stronger winds will exert enough force to counter any disturbance from the motion of the boat.

Availability

The following use vertical wind-vanes: Hasler, RVG, Saye's Rig, Schwingpilot, Windpilot Atlantik/Caribic.

The horizontal vane

How it works

A horizontal or H windvane rotates about a horizontal axis. When it is pointing directly into the wind it stands upright. When the wind strikes it from the side – that is, when the boat is off course – it tilts to one side, Fig 4.1b. What distinguishes this type of vane is the fact that when a course deviation occurs, the wind strikes it over the whole of one face rather than just along the leading edge. As a result, it has a substantially larger effective windvane area. H vanes are therefore able to exert considerably more leverage than V vanes and are said to be about 5.6 times as efficient.

Adjustment

Some horizontal vanes have adjust-able fore-and-aft inclination. The upright position offers maximum effective area for the wind, which is desirable in light air. Inclining the vane aft, away from the wind, as the wind strength increases helps to reduce lateral swinging movements, allowing the gear to operate more smoothly.

Shape

Because a horizontal windvane obtains its force from the wind strik-ing the side of the vane, there is noth-ing to be gained by using anything other than a flat section.

Mounting and removal

Many of today's horizontal vane

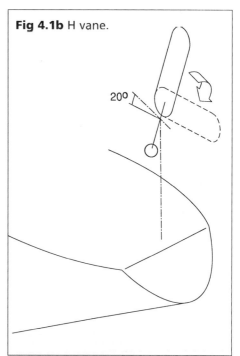

Fig 4.1b H vane.

20°

H vane, Windpilot Pacific Plus double rudder system.

systems use plywood vanes fastened to some kind of mounting bracket. Plywood is a relatively soft material, so to prevent damage in strong winds there should ideally be a large contact area between the mounting bracket and the vane. The vane should also be easy to remove as the lazy skipper will otherwise be tempted to leave it fitted even in harbour, leading to unnecessary wear or breakage when it is not even in use. Many Aries vanes have been left in place for years once the skipper realised that removal entailed disassembling the entire locking device. The Sailomat 601 gear has the windvane inserted into a slotted aluminium tube, an arrangement that provides very little contact area between the mounting bracket and the vane. Monitor vanes are removed by undoing a pair of bolts. The Windpilot Pacific mounting bracket provides a large contact area with the vane and has a slot that allows quick removal of the vane once the locking device has been loosened one complete turn.

Counterweight

A horizontal windvane needs to be perfectly balanced by a counterweight to prevent spurious steering impulses caused by the motion of the boat. This means that the counterweight should be very slightly heavier ($10–30\,\text{g}/\frac{1}{3}–1\,\text{oz}$ heavier is normally sufficient) than the vane it is intended to balance. Some sailors attach rubber bands to the counterweight on traditional servo-pendulum systems to help restore the windvane to its neutral position. While this measure can offset the substantial inertia of the push rod, it does not increase the sensitivity of the system.

Area

Because of its considerably greater efficiency, an H vane can be much smaller than an equivalent V vane. It is possible to change vanes according to wind strength, but this only works if the counterweight is changed at the same time. In any case, modern servo-pendulum gears are sensitive enough that one vane is adequate for the whole range of wind strengths. Almost all manufacturers specify an H vane area of $0.17\,\text{m}^2/1\frac{3}{4}\,\text{ft}^2$ for servo-pendulum gears and $0.25\,\text{m}^2/2\frac{3}{4}\,\text{ft}^2$ for auxiliary rudder systems.

Plywood has several practical advantages as a material for H vanes. It is light, cheap and robust, and a plywood vane can easily be replaced using tools common on most boats. Be prepared to replace the vane. Weigh it and note the result – every replacement vane must weigh exactly the same. A plywood vane can be lightened simply by sawing a piece off. If you must have a larger windvane, especially for light airs, the weight can be kept down by cutting large holes in the vane and covering them with spinnaker cloth.

Tip: A strip of spinnaker cloth (approximately $2.5 \times 80\,\text{cm}/1 \times 31\,\text{in}$) stuck to the upper aft corner of the vane works wonders in light airs. Its fluttering action accentuates the movements of the plywood vane, which can otherwise become a little lethargic in very light conditions.

A horizontal windvane generally offers a smaller effective working surface to the wind and is easily handled and removed. H vanes also require relatively little operating space. They normally have no problem with yawl and ketch rigged yachts and even davits rarely interfere.

A strip of spinnaker cloth stuck to the vane works wonders in light airs.

The linkage

The steering impulse from a wind-vane is transmitted mechanically to the rudder blade of the gear. Depending on the type of system, the vane and blade may be linked by simple push rods, by levers, sheathed cables, lines or toothed or bevel gears. We will deal individually with the different linkage transmissions and how they work later on.

The rudder

The auxiliary rudder or pendulum rudder of a windvane gear effects the course correction either
• Directly (auxiliary rudder system), or
• Indirectly (servo-pendulum and double rudder systems), the deflection of the windvane in the latter case causing the pendulum rudder to swing out sideways and, in turn, pass this motion via lines to the main rudder, where it carries out the corrective movement.

Auxiliary rudder

An auxiliary rudder is an additional steering rudder which makes steering movements independently of the main rudder. Auxiliary rudders may be up to $0.27\,\text{m}^2/3\,\text{ft}^2$ in area. The ratio of main rudder area to auxiliary rudder area should be no greater than 3:1. Bear in mind here that the main rudder area has to be sufficient to steer the boat even under engine. The auxiliary rudder, however, is only called upon to make minor corrections. It does not have the same steering function as the main rudder and can therefore be smaller.

The ratio of main rudder area to auxiliary rudder area is ideally 3:1.

Pendulum rudder

A pendulum rudder generates servo forces by swinging out to one side. These forces are transmitted to the main rudder. The amount of force produced is determined by the length of the pendulum arm from its

Pendulum rudder to main rudder proportions: the lever effect is the key to this system.

Trim tab to main rudder proportion: this system type can make reversing under power awkward.

pivot point to the bottom end of the pendulum rudder. This distance, known as the power leverage (PL), is usually somewhere between 150 and 200 cm/60–80 in. Pendulum rudders are about $0.1\,m^2/1\,ft^2$ in area.

Trim tab

A trim tab pivots sideways to move the trailing edge of the rudder to which it is attached. Trim tabs are normally less than $0.08\,m^2/0.85\,ft^2$ in area and can be attached to main, auxiliary or pendulum rudders.

Pre-balancing the rudder

Pre-balancing a rudder blade, which involves moving the rudder shaft to a position about 20 per cent aft from the leading edge, reduces the force needed to turn the rudder. This effect is the same as the sudden increased weight on the tiller when a dinghy rudder pivots up after touching the bottom. As soon as the rudder drops back into its vertical position, the balance is restored and the load on the tiller drops to almost nothing again.

Almost all modern yachts have a pre-balanced rudder blade. This is a bonus for all types of windvane gears because a more easily turned rudder allows the gear to work properly with weaker windvane steering impulses. The obvious result of this is better light air performance.

If the pre-balancing procedure is overdone and the shaft is positioned between 23 and 25 per cent aft, the rudder blade will be unsettled and will tend to swing out. In extreme cases, the rudder blade may end up turning the windvane instead of the other way around.

Damping

One of the first lessons of helming a boat is to steer as little as possible. Vigorous use of the tiller or wheel to correct the course tends to be ineffective because the boat always turns too far, immediately necessitating another course correction in the opposite direction and leaving a snake wake trailing astern.

An experienced helmsperson, with greater awareness of the behaviour of the boat, keeps steering movements to a minimum, following one of two mental 'steering programmes':

1 He or she tries to steer the optimum upwind course or, given another point of sail, precisely hold a desired compass course. A picture of concentration, our experienced helm studies the wind direction indicator, the sails or the compass closely, giving almost continuous small, occasionally larger, steering impulses to keep yawing and course deviation as small as possible.
2 He or she prefers a more relaxed attitude at the helm, correcting the course rarely and with small movements; the course varies over a greater range of angles.

How a boat responds to the helm is determined chiefly by design; a long-keel boat will always be more sluggish than one with a fin keel and a balanced rudder.

Experienced helms develop an internal 'damping programme' which ensures that, almost without having to think, they are sparing in their use of the rudder. Rudder movements not only turn the boat, they also brake it, so minimising them preserves boat speed as well.

A windvane steering system lacks the wisdom of experience and, unless damped, will always turn the rudder too hard, too far and for too long – that is, oversteer. Damping must therefore be designed into a system to replace its clumsiness with the gift of delicate steering and enable it to equal or even exceed the steering performance of our experienced helm. This can be done.

Principle 1
More damping equals better steering (although obviously not to the point where the system is so well damped that it does not move at all). Conceiving and building a system that properly balances damping and steering is the toughest challenge facing any windvane steering designer. Systems must be powerful, but they must deliver their power in a controlled way.

Principle 2
The less damping there is built into the system, the more additional measures the helmsperson will have to take to offset this steering deficit and cajole the system up to a level where it can cope with a particular boat. This entails not only maintaining perfect sail trim but also reducing canvas early to cut the steering demands placed on the windvane gear. Poorly damped systems make particularly

hard work of reaching and downwind courses and often surrender full control to the elements.

Principle 3

With no damping at all, self-steering is only possible if sail trim and sail area are so perfectly set that the boat steers straight ahead entirely of its own accord. Of course if your boat tracks along a straight line all on its own you might as well jettison the windvane gear altogether. Completely undamped systems can steer properly at just a few specific wind angles and are only really suitable as an aid to steering.

A well-balanced windvane gear will always put up the most satisfactory steering performance; it is best equipped to steer the boat under all sailing and weather conditions. Indeed, a good gear of this nature inevitably steers better than even an alert helmsperson because the continuous damping of all rudder movements keeps yawing angles permanently small and, with a windvane, optimum heading with respect to the wind is guaranteed all the time. Such a gear can be rated as providing effective steering.

The term 'effective steering' is used to indicate the range of a particular windvane steering system. What use is a gear that can manage only 70 per cent of given conditions or courses if it always retires precisely when manual steering appeals least – that is, in heavy weather?

Squeezing satisfactory steering performance from a poorly equipped windvane gear means extra work for the crew. Eventually it makes more sense to steer by hand than keep running round the boat tweaking everything to prop up the gear.

Damping can be provided:

- At the windvane
- At the linkage
- At the rudder

Damping at the windvane

V vane

A V vane rotating about a vertical axis (weathervane principle) is deflected very little by the wind – at most by the amount in degrees of the deviation from course – and there is almost always wind flowing along both sides of the vane. This gives a high level of damping.

H vane

An H vane rotating about a horizontal axis can be subject to extreme deflection by the wind, in some cases through as much as 90°, whereupon it hits its lateral end stops. The wind acts on one side of the vane only, and the amount of deflection is determined by wind strength rather than wind angle. The result is poor damping, since the windvane only begins to return to its centred position once the boat is back on course and the wind can reach the lee side of the vane and push it back upright. The vane therefore continues the steering impulse for too long – that is, is damped too late. Inclining the horizontal axis – that is, bringing it closer to the vertical axis – reduces the sensitivity of the system; the magnitude of the course correction signal declines because flow reaches the lee side earlier and more quickly, slowing the deflection of the vane.

The indispensable contribution of Marcel Gianoli, one of the pioneers already mentioned, to the development of windvane steering was to identify 20° aft as the optimum angle of inclination for the horizontal axis.

Characteristics of the three types of windvane

	H vane	V vane	H vane, 20°
Force	large	small	moderate
Travel	large	small	moderate
Position in the wind	unsettled	stable	moderate
Space requirement/ turning radius	small	large	moderate
Sensitivity	high	low	moderate
Damping	slight	great	moderate

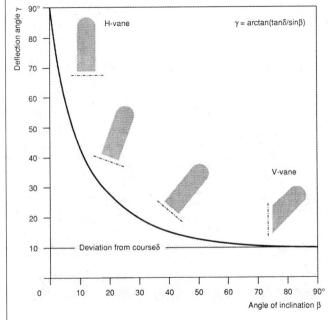

$$\gamma = \arctan(\tan\delta/\sin\beta)$$

Fig 4.1 An H vane rotating about a precisely horizontal axis can be deflected up to 90° to one side before wind reaches the other side of the vane to slow or damp the lateral movement. The steering impulse is too strong.

A V vane rotating about a vertical axis can be deflected by no more than 10°, ie the amount in degrees of the deviation from course. The steering signal is too weak.

An H vane rotating about an axis inclined by 20° strikes the optimum balance between good steering impulse and good damping.

Virtually all H vane gears make use of this feature. There are two principal categories:

1 H vanes which are fixed in this 20° position (Atoms, Fleming, Monitor, Mustafa, Navik, Cap Horn, Sailomat); and
2 H vanes on an axis of 20° but which are freely adjustable, permitting them to be matched to different wind strengths in the interests of better steering – for example, more upright in lighter winds, more steeply inclined in heavier winds (Aries, BWS, Hydrovane, Windpilot Pacific). Adjusting the angle of the windvane changes the leverage available to the wind, so an upright vane gives a stronger signal for light air on account of the longer lever, and an aft inclined vane gives a weaker signal on account of the shorter lever. The leverage exercised by the windvane declines as it is inclined aft.

Damping at the linkage

The steering impulse from the wind-vane is translated by a gear or rod linkage into a lateral rotation of the rudder.

Damping or manual adjustment:

1 Auxiliary rudder with V vane

No additional measures necessary since the inherent damping of a V vane is sufficient. Steering force can thus be transmitted via spur gears or toothed wheels in a 1:1 ratio (Windpilot Atlantik/Caribic).

2 Auxiliary rudder with H vane

Essential, as the rudder angle set by the windvane is a function of wind strength rather than wind angle and can thus become excessive, produc-ing oversteering, in heavy air. The rudder angle can be changed and reduced manually at the gearbox to cut back the power of the H vane (Hydrovane).

3 Trim tab

Desirable, but complicated by the need to transmit the signals to an additional, remote shaft (trim tab shaft). The restoring forces produced by the auxiliary or main rudder to which the trim tab attaches usually furnish adequate damping. Manual adjustment of windvane to push rod signal transmission makes setting up the system easier (BWS).

4 Servo-pendulum gear

(see Yaw damping, Chapter 5)
Elaborate damping using a bevel gear in a step-down ratio of 2:1. This kind of damping is designated auto-matic damping because every steer-ing impulse causes the pendulum arm to swing out in a precisely defined manner, the pendulum rud-der simultaneously being brought back parallel to the centreline (Aries, Monitor, Windpilot Pacific). There are four main approaches to servo-pendulum gear design in this respect:

- Bevel gear – segment gear which only needs to cover a fairly limited range of operation between the two steering line guide tubes, mounted on both sides at the bot-tom of the gear, which restrict the lateral travel of the pendulum arm and make it impossible to raise (Aries, Monitor).

- A 360° bevel gear – complete gear in which the gearwheels mesh over a pivoting range of 270°, allowing the pendulum arm to be raised up laterally out of the water (Windpilot Pacific); 2:1 bevel gear linkages are now standard with all the major servo-pendulum system manufacturers (Aries, Monitor, Windpilot Pacific). The 2:1 trans-mission doubles the force of the steering impulse from the wind-vane while halving the lateral travel of the pendulum arm.

- Systems using other mechanical arrangements to control the move-ment of the pendulum rudder (Cap Horn, Atoms).

- Systems in which the linkage per-forms no damping function.

5 Double rudder systems

These rely on the damping of the servo-pendulum system they incor-porate. The categories are:

- Servo-pendulum systems with automatic bevel gear yaw damp-ing and angling of the pendulum rudder shaft aft by 10°, in combi-nation with the inherent damping of the auxiliary rudder (Windpilot Pacific Plus);

- Servo-pendulum systems damped by angling the pendulum rudder shaft aft 34°, combined with the natural controlling influence of the auxiliary rudder (Stayer/Sailomat 3040).

Damping at the rudder

1 Auxiliary rudder
This steers directly and is reset/damped by the pressure of the water flowing past.

2 Pendulum rudder
Angling the pendulum rudder shaft aft achieves a damping effect in the water similar to that of an H vane in air. Given this angled shaft, the pendulum rudder can only swing out a certain distance before the force of the water starts to push it back in. The alternatives are:

- Vertical shaft and bevel gear linkage (Aries, Monitor);
- Shaft angled aft by 34° for damping, no bevel gear linkage. These systems require manual adjustment of windvane to push rod signal transmission characteristics to properly set the proportional relationship between the H vane steering impulse and the lateral pendulum rudder movement (Sailomat 601);
- Bevel gear linkage, shaft angled aft by 10° (Windpilot Pacific).

3 Double rudder
See previous section.

A windvane gear with properly balanced damping properties will always turn the rudder by exactly the amount required, preventing oversteering. The feedback between the position of the rudder and that of the windvane ensures the steering pressure is only increased until the vane signals that the boat has begun to react and return to course. As the vane begins to move back towards its upright position, the pendulum rudder reduces the steering force on the main rudder and returns to the centre.

This may seem rather complicated on paper, but fortunately it is not necessary to understand the science in order to appreciate the perfect steering that a well-damped windvane gear will bring to your boat. Such a gear will also be very insistent in its criticism of your sail trim – if it never seems to be centred and is always working off to one side, you can be sure that something needs attention.

Every crew will realise sooner or later that it pays to act on these hints: correcting sail trim or adjusting the main rudder to relieve the pendulum rudder not only appeases the gear, it also improves boat speed. Systems with bevel gear linkages pull on the main rudder with gradually increasing force until feedback via the windvane returns the pendulum arm to its central position; oversteering is impossible.

A less well damped windvane steering system demands an attentive crew, particularly in changeable or worsening wind conditions. The steering system will have to be helped along by reefing early and reducing motion (staysail). Operating a system of this kind is taxing, especially for those with only limited knowledge of the processes at work in a servo-dynamic steering system. Such systems do not provide effective steering.

• 5 •

Types of system

Windvane-only systems

The steering impulse and steering force from the windvane are transmitted directly to the tiller via lines and there is no servo or additional rudder blade.

Steering impulse   = wind
Steering force   = wind
Steering element   = main rudder
Power leverage (PL) = 0 cm

This type of system was originally developed for model yachts. It is not very efficient and generates too little force to steer a sailing boat in all weather conditions.

Francis Chichester's first self-steering gear 'Miranda' was a windvane-only system with a $4\,m^2/43\,ft^2$ vane and a $12\,kg/26\frac{1}{2}\,lb$ counterweight. This system was not particularly successful, as we mentioned earlier, since it was unable to generate sufficient steering force to control the tiller properly.

Windvane-only systems can be used on smaller boats (up to 6 m) to help with upwind steering. Off the wind and in any kind of sea the forces generated by the vane are too low.

Windvane-only systems: QME, Windpilot Nordsee I. Production ceased on systems like this many years ago. They are mentioned only to give the reader a complete picture.

Auxiliary rudder systems

An auxiliary rudder system is a discrete steering unit which steers the boat independently of the main rudder. The windvane turns a rudder blade on a rigid shaft directly via a linkage, maintaining the corrective rudder movement until the boat returns to the desired course.

Steering impulse   = wind
Steering force   = wind
Steering element   = auxiliary
                       rudder
Power leverage (PL) = 0 cm

The main rudder is fixed in place and used to fine tune the gear. It counters weather helm, allowing the auxiliary rudder to concentrate solely on actual course corrections. Auxiliary rudder systems are only effective if the ratio of the area of the main rudder blade to that of the auxiliary rudder blade is no greater than 3:1. This ratio is easily calculated for any known main rudder dimensions using the auxiliary rudder blade dimensions given in the specifications of the individual systems.

The steering force produced by auxiliary rudder systems is limited by the lack of any servo-assistance, and they are unable to provide effective steering on larger boats. Windpilot auxiliary rudder systems

Fig 5.1 V vane only.

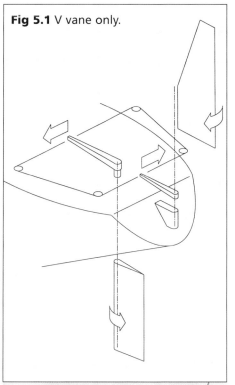

Fig 5.2 H vane only.

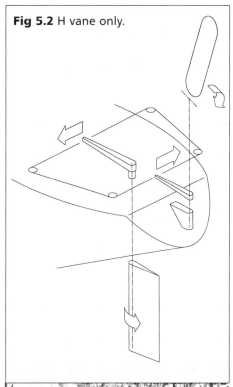

V vane only: Windpilot Nordsee on board a 5 m/16 ft Van de Stadt design.

H vane only: QME windvane. This acts more as a steering aid than a full self-steering system.

Fig 5.3 V vane auxiliary rudder system.

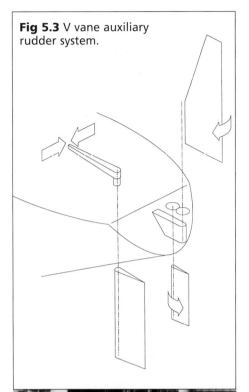

Fig 5.4 H vane auxiliary rudder system.

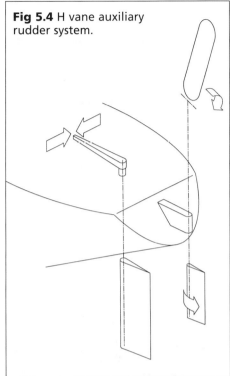

This Windpilot auxiliary rudder system is suitable for boats up to 11 m/36 ft in length.

The Hydrovane auxiliary rudder system: the H vane generates more power than the Atlantik V vane.

of the Nordsee and Atlantik ranges were used successfully on boats of up to approximately 11 m/36 ft, but beyond this they could function only as an aid to steering. For this reason, Windpilot retired them in 1985 and moved on to other systems.

Hydrovane auxiliary rudder systems are recommended for steering boats of up to 15 m/50 ft. The cut-off point with respect to 'effective steering' is probably somewhat lower than this, though, because the systems are not servo-assisted and the ratio of auxiliary rudder area to main rudder area on a larger boat would be rather unfavourable.

Effective steering

We made brief reference to this term in the previous chapter. It is used here to express whether a windvane gear is capable of reliably steering a boat of a particular length in virtually all sailing conditions, or is just an aid to steering up to a certain wind strength, sea state and range of apparent wind angles. As a rating of the capabilities of a windvane steering system it is of fundamental importance; a steering gear that cannot do its job properly is no good to anybody.

Any rating of a steering gear should of course be considered in the context of the type of sailing the gear is likely to be used for. A system that is only reliable for upwind sailing, for instance, might be perfectly acceptable to the weekend and holiday sailor. However, the priorities aboard blue water yachts are rather different: steering by hand for days on end will often exhaust a small crew and bring a premature end to the voyage.

Categories of auxiliary rudder systems

Auxiliary rudder with V vane: The vane in a V vane operated auxiliary rudder system (eg Windpilot Atlantik) turns the rudder directly via opposed toothed gears in a ratio of 1:1. The damping characteristics are good. Systems of this type are suitable for boats of up to 11 m/36 ft.

Auxiliary rudder with H vane: These systems (eg Hydrovane) have less effective damping than V vane operated auxiliary rudder systems. To resolve this, they have a reduction gear that provides three options for the amount of turn transmitted to the rudder. They do, however, produce rather more effective steering force than a V vane and can therefore be used on larger boats.

The Hydrovane linkage has step-down gearing for better damping.

The advantages of auxiliary rudder systems

Because the auxiliary rudder functions totally independently of the main rudder, it makes an effective emergency rudder. This is a useful safety feature, particularly on modern fin keel yachts where the balanced rudder has no skeg to protect it. The additional lateral area of the auxiliary rudder right at the very back of the boat not only helps to calm the motion of the boat in heavy seas, but also reduces weather helm.

The simple, solid construction of auxiliary rudder gears gives them a long working life. They can only really suffer serious damage if the boat is rammed hard from astern – and even then there is the consolation that steering gears cost much less to repair than the transoms they are mounted on!

Operating procedure:
- Bring the boat on to course
- Fix the tiller in position
- Turn the windvane to face into the wind
- Connect the windvane to the auxiliary rudder
- Fine tune the course using the main rudder

The disadvantages of auxiliary rudder systems

Nobody ever stood on a harbour wall and admired the beauty of their auxiliary rudder gear. The systems are tall, bulky and heavy, and the extreme end of a boat, particularly a small one, is not the place to add 30–45 kg/66–100 lb of extra weight.

The limited steering force obtainable without any servo-assistance means that this type of system is unable in practice to provide effective steering for longer boats (see above).

The auxiliary rudder is generally fixed amidships when not in use. Here it impairs the vessel's manoeuvrability and increases its turning circle. Curiously this apparent drawback is actually a bonus for some: the additional lateral area behind the main rudder makes boats with long keels more obedient to the helm when reversing because it partially offsets propeller throw which tries to push the stern sideways.

The large windvanes of auxiliary rudder systems makes them awkward to operate on ketch or yawl rigged boats when the mizzen is in use.

Installation

Auxiliary rudder systems can be mounted either on the centre of the transom or offset to one side, for example to avoid a swim ladder. As

Offset mounting next to a swim ladder. The Viking ships also had their steering system positioned to one side.

This BWS-Taurus system would be better with a V-shaped bracket at the bottom.

Offset mounting next to an outboard rudder. The minimum distance to the main rudder is 30 cm/12 in.

the Vikings discovered a long time ago, mounting the rudder to one side has only a very minor effect on steering performance. The rudders on their longships were always mounted on the starboard side and the helmsman steered with his back facing to port.

Considerable lateral forces act on the auxiliary rudder in certain sea conditions, so its attachment to the transom must be strong and solid. Traditional overhanging transoms will require the gear to be supported at the bottom by a V-shaped bracket. An angle flange at the bottom is sufficient for modern forward-raked transoms.

The auxiliary rudder should be at least 20–30 cm/8–12 in behind the main rudder (this can be a problem on modern open-transom boats where the rudder is positioned far aft). Any less than this and the auxiliary rudder blade will be in the turbulent wash of the main rudder,

which prevents it from bringing its full force to bear and consequently impairs the efficiency of the system.

Off-centre mounting on boats with an outboard main rudder is only practical if the lateral distance between the main and auxiliary rudders is at least 30 cm/12 in. Such a large offset reduces the efficiency of the system when going to weather because some of the auxiliary rudder area will lift out of the water on one tack when the boat heels.

Auxiliary rudder systems function best on traditional boats with long keels and big overhanging transoms. The auxiliary rudder is so far behind the main rudder in boats of this design that it encounters hardly any turbulent wash, allowing it to achieve maximum efficiency. The large distance from the main rudder also gives it considerable leverage.

Auxiliary rudder system manufacturers: Windpilot and Hydrovane.

Trim-tab-on-auxiliary-rudder systems

How they work

The steering impulse from the wind-vane is passed to a trim tab attached to the trailing edge of the auxiliary rudder. As the trim tab is pivoted out to one side it pushes the trailing edge of the auxiliary rudder to the opposite side. The movement of the auxiliary rudder effects the course correction. The main rudder is fixed in place and used for fine trim in the same way as with a simple auxiliary rudder gear.

Steering impulse = wind
Steering force = water
Steering element = auxiliary rudder
Power leverage (PL) = approx. 20 cm/8 in

Trim tabs are very small, normally no more than 20 per cent of the area of the auxiliary rudder blade.

There are two advantages to diverting the steering impulse from the windvane via a trim tab on its way to the auxiliary rudder:

1 Since the trim tab it has to turn is very small, the windvane can also be small.
2 The distance between the trim tab axis and the auxiliary rudder axis generates a servo effect which gives this type of system more steering power than a simple auxiliary rudder gear. This is analogous to the way a small trim tab on the trailing edge of an aeroplane wing is able to turn the whole flap and steer the plane.

Length of lever = servo force: The separation between the axis of the auxil-iary rudder and the axis of the trim tab accounts for the leverage that creates the servo effect. The distance between the two axes is usually about 20 cm/8 in, so the maximum achievable servo effect with this type of system is relatively small. The servo effect can be enhanced to a certain extent by pre-balancing the rudder, but the achievable steering force will never be very large because the trim tab is unable to turn the auxil-iary rudder any more than about 10°.

Trim tab operated steering gears represent an important development in the evolution of the windvane steering system. Using the trim tab to amplify the force generated by the vane was the first step towards smaller windvanes and higher steering forces. Today this type of gear is outdated and, as we shall see, wind-vane steering technology has moved on.

Advantages and disadvantages

Advantages
Smaller windvane but somewhat greater steering force; functions independently of the main rudder; can be used as an emergency rudder. These systems also have all the advantages of simple auxiliary rudder gears.

Disadvantages
Even larger, bulkier and heavier than simple auxiliary rudder systems. A particular disadvantage of these systems is that they make manoeuvring under engine even more difficult; an auxiliary rudder with a trim tab is more or less impossible to fix in place, so motoring in reverse is no fun at all. It is not easy to fit a yaw-damping device to systems of this type, so most sailors manage without.

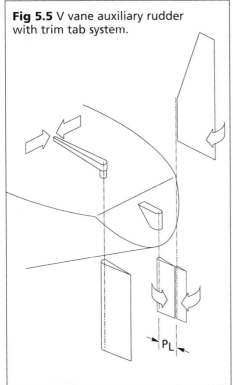

Fig 5.5 V vane auxiliary rudder with trim tab system.

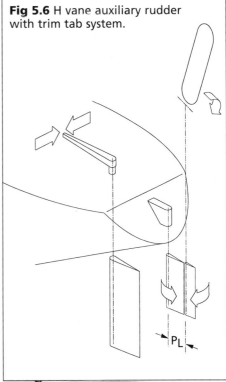

Fig 5.6 H vane auxiliary rudder with trim tab system.

An RVG V vane auxiliary rudder with trim tab system fitted on the 10 m/33 ft glassfibre *Sy* moored in Palma de Mallorca.

A Mustafa H vane auxiliary rudder with trim tab system – the dinosaur among the vanes.

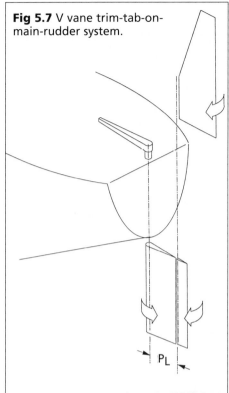

Fig 5.7 V vane trim-tab-on-main-rudder system.

P_L

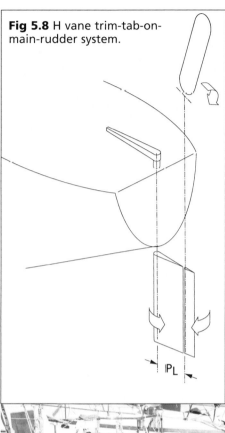

Fig 5.8 H vane trim-tab-on-main-rudder system.

P_L

V vane trim-tab-on-main-rudder system, custom-built for a 10 m/32 ft Olle Enderlein design.

H vane trim-tab-on-main-rudder system, Windpilot Pacific custom-built for a Danish Kaskelot.

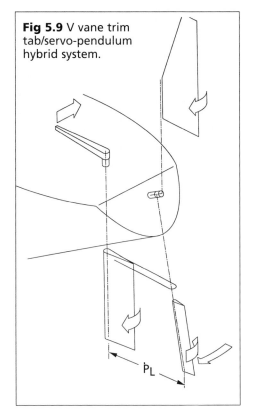

Fig 5.9 V vane trim tab/servo-pendulum hybrid system.

PL

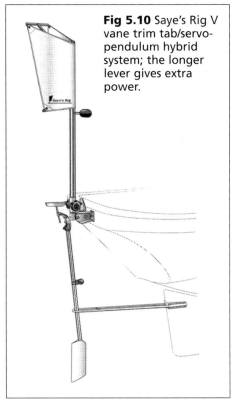

Fig 5.10 Saye's Rig V vane trim tab/servo-pendulum hybrid system; the longer lever gives extra power.

Installation

Auxiliary-rudder-with-trim-tab gears need to be mounted on the centre of the transom. Some sea conditions can place substantial loads on both the system; the transom and the mounting must be very robust to support the considerable weight of the gear. V vane systems have a relatively large turning radius, so H vanes – which are more easily kept clear of mizzen masts – are more suitable for ketch- and yawl-rigged boats.

Trim-tab-on-auxiliary-rudder system manufacturers: **1** V vane: RVG. **2** H vane: Auto Helm, BWS Taurus, Mustafa.

Trim-tab-on-main-rudder systems

How they work

The trim tab is mounted on the trailing edge of the main rudder, moving it directly.

Steering impulse   = wind
Steering force   = water
Steering element   = main rudder
Power leverage (PL) = 30–50 cm/
                  12–20 in

Popular in the early days of wind-vane steering, this configuration did well on boats with long keels and an outboard rudder and was suitable for DIY construction. Bernard Moit-essier used the simplest of all trim tab gears on *Joshua*. The trim tab was

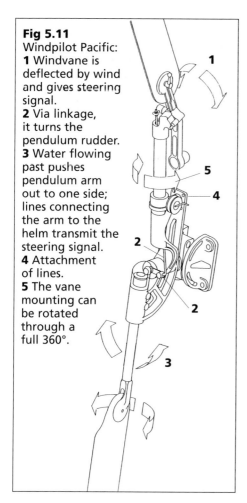

Fig 5.11
Windpilot Pacific:
1 Windvane is deflected by wind and gives steering signal.
2 Via linkage, it turns the pendulum rudder.
3 Water flowing past pushes pendulum arm out to one side; lines connecting the arm to the helm transmit the steering signal.
4 Attachment of lines.
5 The vane mounting can be rotated through a full 360°.

once a stronghold of trim tab systems, has seen a move towards modern servo-pendulum gears.

Trim-tab-on-main-rudder designs have many drawbacks: providing them with yaw damping is difficult, the trim tab causes problems with manoeuvring under engine, and any kind of mass production is all but impossible because the key parameters vary so much from boat to boat. Virtually every yacht design has a unique main rudder with its own rudder post angle and balance proportions, and each one consequently requires a unique trim tab. This system has all but disappeared now.

Trim-tab-on-main-rudder system manufacturers: Atlas, Auto-Steer, Hasler, Saye's Rig, Windpilot.

The Saye's Rig is a hybrid pendulum/trim tab system in which the power leverage (PL) is increased by a bracket attached directly to the main rudder.

Servo-pendulum systems

Since this is the most popular system today, we shall devote the next few pages to a detailed look at its various features.

How they work

The windvane rotates the blade of the pendulum rudder via a linkage. The blade is mounted on a shaft which is able to swing from side to side like a pendulum (hence the name). When the blade is rotated, the force of the water flowing past pushes against it and swings it out to one side. The shaft on which the pendulum rudder swings is connected to the tiller (or wheel) via lines, so the lateral movement of the pendulum rudder is

connected to the trailing edge of the main rudder and it sat on an extension of the vertical windvane shaft.

These systems are prone to oversteering and generally have no yaw damping, so they will only work well on an optimally balanced boat. Trim must be close to perfect so that the boat can be steered with very small movements. Under some circumstances this can mean drastically reducing sail area to enable the steering system to stay roughly on course.

The absence of yaw damping on most gears of this type makes them hard work. As a result, even France, translated into a pulling force on the tiller (or turning force on the wheel) which effects the course correction. Once the boat is back on course, the windvane returns the pendulum rudder blade to the centre.

Steering impulse   = wind
Steering force   = water
Steering element   = main rudder
Power leverage (PL) = up to 200 cm/
                      80 in

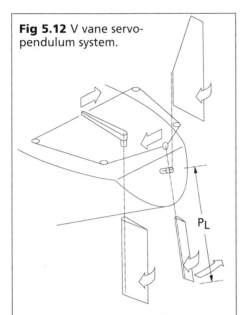

Fig 5.12 V vane servo-pendulum system.

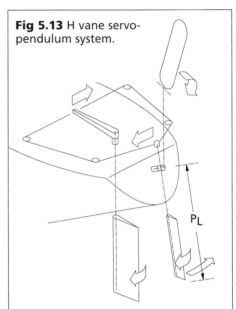

Fig 5.13 H vane servo-pendulum system.

This Windpilot Pacific V vane servo-pendulum system MKI (1969), is made of stainless steel.

The traditional Monitor H vane servo-pendulum system.

The enormous power leverage of the servo-pendulum design compared with other gears clearly reflects the considerable steering and servo forces it is able to generate.

The servo principle

Imagine you are standing at the stern of your boat doing 6 knots holding a $2\,m/6\frac{1}{2}\,ft$ long wooden plank in the water. Align the plank directly on the centreline and you can just about hold it with two fingers. Rotate it slightly, however, and it swings powerfully to one side (your shoulder joint represents the pendulum axis).

Using this principle, the hydrodynamic force of the water flowing past can be harnessed to generate a tensile force of up to $300\,kg/660\,lb$. This explains how servo-pendulum systems are able properly to steer large, heavy boats: not only does a bigger boat require more steering force, it

also inherently produces greater hydrodynamic force for the steering gear to exploit.

Yaw damping

A sailing yacht with nobody at the helm is an inherently unstable system, as it will immediately turn towards the wind until the sails flog. A sailing yacht with a helmsperson/autopilot/windvane gear in control is a stable system. The difference between these two states, which amounts to nothing more than the load on the rudder, may be very small or very large depending on sail trim, weather conditions and the characteristics of the boat. Sometimes a couple of fingers on the wheel are enough to keep the boat on course, but on other occasions the helm can be strenuous work.

The enormous potential force of servo-pendulum gears is also their

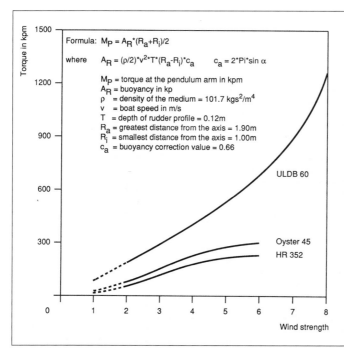

Formula: $M_P = A_R{}^*(R_a+R_i)/2$

where $A_R = (\rho/2)^*v^2{}^*T^*(R_a-R_i)^*c_a$ $c_a = 2^*Pi^*\sin\alpha$

M_P = torque at the pendulum arm in kpm
A_R = buoyancy in kp
ρ = density of the medium = 101.7 kgs^2/m^4
v = boat speed in m/s
T = depth of rudder profile = 0.12m
R_a = greatest distance from the axis = 1.90m
R_i = smallest distance from the axis = 1.00m
c_a = buoyancy correction value = 0.66

Fig 5.14 This figure shows how the torque at the pendulum arm of a servo-pendulum gear on a displacement boat reaches a natural limit defined by the maximum speed of the boat. ULDBs have no such limit because the boat speed can rise rapidly during surfing. The formula is applied here to a Windpilot Pacific gear with a 12 x 90 cm/4.8 x 36 in rudder blade and a standard power leverage (PL) of 190 cm/76 in.

main problem: unless the force transmitted to the main rudder can be regulated in some way, there is a danger that rudder movements will be too large or too prolonged, leading to oversteering.

Consider how an experienced helm steers. He or she knows that delicate rudder movements are sufficient for course corrections and would never steer with big or vigorous tiller movements. Abrupt, sweeping movements of the helm make it very difficult to judge the boat's exact course, and consequently cause oversteering. Not only that, but unnecessarily sharp rudder movements are also bad for boat speed.

Alternatively, consider the blade of a setting propeller (eg Max Prop) which, in its sailing position, is stationary in the wake of the keel. If it receives a mechanical impulse, it begins to spin endlessly around the shaft, stopping only once it has been

reset. In this analogy, the propeller blade represents the pendulum rudder, the prop-shaft is the pendulum rudder axis, and the windvane provides the mechanical impulse.

If the steering impulse from the windvane was transmitted directly to the pendulum rudder without any kind of braking at all, the pendulum arm would swing out too far to one side, possibly even lifting out of the water, until the wind delivered a steering impulse in the opposite direction. This wide a range of movement would require excessively long lines to transmit the correction to the main rudder and would turn the rudder too far, resulting in oversteering.

Yaw damping in a servo-pendulum gear basically amounts to limiting the lateral travel of the pendulum arm. A balanced system combining a damped windvane and a bevel gear with a step-down ratio of 2:1 is able

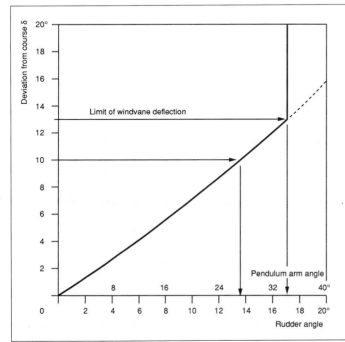

Fig 5.15 Windpilot Pacific: Rudder angle and pendulum arm angle as a function of the deviation from course for a windvane rotating about a 20° inclined axis.

A deviation from course of 10° causes the pendulum arm to swing out 27°, which turns the main rudder by a maximum of 13°. The servo-pendulum gear oversteers only slightly (10° deviation, 13° main rudder movement). This explains the good steering performance of such systems.

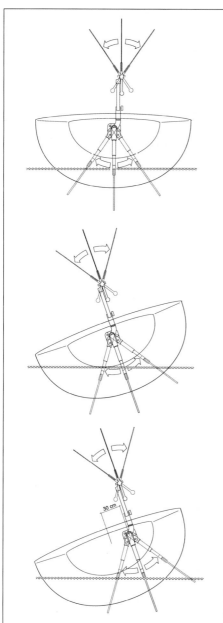

Fig 5.16 Working range of a servo-pendulum system with bevel gear linkage.
a) no incline – pendulum rudder in water
b) inclined – pendulum rudder in water
c) inclined, offset mounting – pendulum rudder lifts out of water

to do this. There is also a second, more critical reason for limiting the lateral swinging range of the pendulum arm: the maximum heeling angle of a sailing boat is about 30°, so the maximum possible working range of the pendulum rudder has to be no more than about 28° to ensure that the combined effect of heel and a large rudder movement does not lift it out of the water to windward. Mounting a servo-pendulum gear offset to one side would obviously accentuate this problem, further reducing the useful working range, and is therefore not at all advisable (see Fig 5.16). Most course corrections involve the pendulum rudder swinging out to windward; this is the movement that directs the main rudder to bear away, and bearing away is by far the most commonly required course correction.

The steering impulse from the windvane swings the pendulum arm out no more than 28°. Every time the windvane rotates the pendulum rudder blade, the pendulum arm is pushed out to one side, simultaneously rotating the rudder back parallel to the centreline (but so as to remain offset laterally from the centreline). This arrangement keeps the maximum steering line travel down to about 25 cm/10 in and effectively prevents oversteering.

The state of the art in servo-pendulum gears today is a horizontal vane, inclined by 20° (see Chapter 4), acting through a bevel gear with a step-down ratio of 2:1. Aries, Monitor, and Windpilot Pacific use identical configurations in this respect.

A servo-pendulum system with a bevel gear provides perfect steering and always delivers precisely the

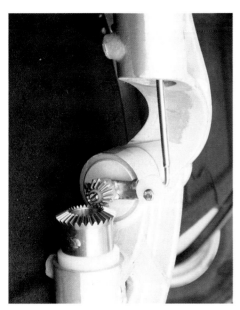

Windpilot Pacific 360° bevel gear linkage ratio 2:1.

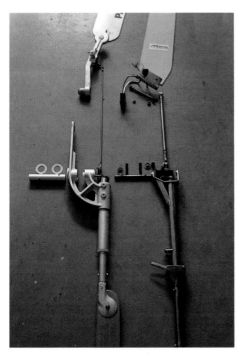

The Windpilot Pacific (left) and Monitor are identical in design, but have substantially different dimensions of pushrod, pendulum axle diameter and pendulum carriage.

force required to bring the boat back to the desired course. If attitudes to sail trim become more relaxed, the gear automatically generates greater pressure on the main rudder which is then adjusted more forcefully.

Servo-pendulum systems that do not have yaw damping are demanding of the crew, placing undue emphasis on balance, sail trim and the idiosyncrasies of the boat. Wind and sea conditions can also provoke an unacceptable deterioration in steering performance.

The push rod

The steering impulse from the windvane is transmitted via a vertical push rod to the linkage where, after being amplified by the bevel gear, it effects the lateral adjustment of the pendulum rudder. The forces encountered here are generally quite moderate, and the key is to ensure that the impulse is sensitive, prompt and reliable even in light air. Manufacturers have tended in the past to overestimate considerably the loads on the push rod and consequently to overbuild it. Aries use a chunky cast push rod which weighs in at over $1\,kg/2\frac{1}{4}\,lb$, and Monitor's component is $450\,g/1\,lb$; the more modern Windpilot Pacific manages with an $8 \times 1\,mm/0.3 \times 0.04\,in$ stainless steel tube which weighs only $143\,g/5\,oz$, and has proved its strength on thousands of boats over the last 12 years. Not surprisingly, such different designs give very different steering performances.

Remember: The push rod is one of the factors that determine light air steering characteristics; it must be as light as possible and no stronger than necessary.

Steering force transmission

Lines are used to transmit the force generated by the pendulum rudder to the boat. The steering lines in a conventional system (Aries, Monitor) are attached to the pendulum arm itself and start at the bottom of the gear. From there the two lines (one on each side) are guided through three blocks up to deck level, where two more blocks each lead them to the tiller or wheel. These systems therefore require ten blocks and correspondingly long steering lines. Modern designs, in contrast, have the pendulum arm extended upwards, enabling the steering lines to start at deck level. The number of blocks required is reduced from ten to just four, and the steering lines are also correspondingly shorter. Care must be taken with modern systems to ensure that the steering lines from the pendulum arm are initially led parallel to the vessel's transom. Although a certain deviation from parallel is tolerable, the effective line travel will be reduced if the transmission angle is too unfavourable. Larger boats in particular need the full line travel.

To facilitate the use of this type of system on double-enders and extreme 'sugar-scoop' sterns, the Windpilot Pacific design includes a cross member with fastening points at each end for the steering line blocks. This option is not available with the Sailomat 601.

Steering line routeing on a double-ender.

Short transmission path to the tiller with the Windpilot Pacific. The steering lines start at deck level.

A servo-pendulum system will only work well if the force from the gear is transmitted smoothly to the main rudder. Arrangements with shorter transmission paths (line lengths) and fewer turning blocks accordingly deliver better steering results. Put another way, the longer the transmission paths and the longer the lines, the greater the transmission losses will be. Slack or stretchy lines and stiffness in the main rudder reduce the efficiency of the system. A servo-pendulum system is only as good as the quality of the force transmission.

Steering line travel

The amount by which the steering lines move as the gear goes from centre to lock, the maximum line travel, is only about 25 cm/10 in for a servo-pendulum system with bevel gear yaw damping. Ineffective force transmission, slack, stretchy lines or excessively long transmission paths can quickly eat into this figure. Given a combination of factors, it is possible that the maximum line travel could fall to as low as 10 cm/4 in. A gear with as restricted a range as this will demonstrate its inefficiency at the slightest opportunity; sooner or later the rudder will lose control.

A good servo-pendulum gear can generate up to 300 kg/660 lb of steering force – enough to keep anything up to a 60-footer happily on course. The key to actually achieving good steering performance from a servo-pendulum system is, quite simply, the quality of the force transmission arrangement.

Tip: The effective line travel, and hence the magnitude of corrective rudder movements the gear can make, can be increased by moving the centred position of the windvane more to leeward (which is easy to do by adjusting the tiller mounting or wheel adaptor). This method relies on the fact that almost all windvane gear course corrections are bear-away movements. It may be the only way in extreme conditions of achieving sufficiently large rudder angles.

Transmission to a tiller

Boats with tiller steering provide ideal circumstances for the transmission of the steering forces. Aft cock-

The 25 cm/10 in steering line travel demonstrated here on an Aries, but identical on both the Monitor and Windpilot Pacific.

Windpilot Pacific tiller fitting and chain link. The connection can be released easily for manual helming.

pits allow the transmission paths to be kept short and the attachment point of the steering lines on the tiller can be moved around or even, as is found on some lighter or faster boats, be mounted on an adjustable track. The steering lines are preferably attached to the tiller by a short length of chain, one link of which latches between the two teeth of the tiller fitting. Some systems use an arrangement in which the lines are fastened to the tiller with comb cleats, but this is not a particularly practical arrangement.

The tiller fitting is mounted at a point about six-tenths of the way along the tiller, that is, just aft of the area normally held for steering. The path of the steering lines out to the blocks at the side of the cockpit is angled aft slightly so as to follow the turning radius of the tiller. One advantage of this is that the lines always assume the correct tension when the chain is latched into the tiller fitting and the gear engaged.

The lines used to transmit the steering force must be pre-stretched rope. They should not be set too tight, however, as this causes excessive bearing friction in the turning blocks and reduces the efficiency of steering force transmission to the tiller. Bearing friction can be countered by using ball-bearing blocks on the steering lines. Other factors that adversely affect the efficiency of transmission include too many turning blocks, stretchy or excessively long steering lines and stiffness in the main rudder.

Braided, pre-stretched 8 mm/10 in diameter rope makes very good steering lines. The breaking strain is well above the loads that the lines will actually be exposed to, so stretch is minimal. It is a good idea to end-for-end the lines every so often on longer voyages so that the wear from turning blocks etc is not always concentrated in the same spots.

Fine-trimming with tiller steering

The chain latch arrangement makes it easy to fine-trim the boat's course when the steering gear is in use, and also enables the crew to disconnect it instantaneously if necessary (eg for emergency manoeuvring). Once the chain has been disconnected from the tiller, the gear has no influence on steering, and just follows along behind the boat like an obedient dog. Since the gear does not disturb the helm at all, there is no need to remove the windvane.

Transmission to mechanical wheel steering

The transmission of steering force to a wheel is somewhat less efficient because the transmission path – from the gear to the wheel and from there via the wheel-steering mechanism to the rudder quadrant and the rudder itself – is longer. Obviously transmission losses are higher, so the effective line travel (25 cm/10 in) is reduced.

Practically every boat over 11 m/35 ft now has wheel steering. The reason for this is that the main rudder is too large to be managed comfortably by the helmsperson without some kind of step-down gear. That said, many boats have wheel steering simply because it has become fashionable. Wheels take up more of the cockpit, and many boats that have them would be better steered with a tiller.

Modern wheel-steering systems transmit the steering force mechanically to the rudder quadrant through sheathed cables. The average wheel has a diameter of about 60 cm/2 ft and goes from lock to lock in about 2.5 turns. Almost all servo-pendulum system manufacturers design their wheel adaptors around this standard. Wheel adaptors are, with few exceptions, around 16 cm/6½ in diameter (ie around 53 cm/21 in circumference). Given these dimensions it should be clear that even under perfect transmission conditions with no loss at all, a steering line travel of 25 cm/10 in amounts to slightly less than half a revolution of the wheel.

All wheels are designed assuming the same amount of steering force input by the helmsperson. This means that larger diameter wheels

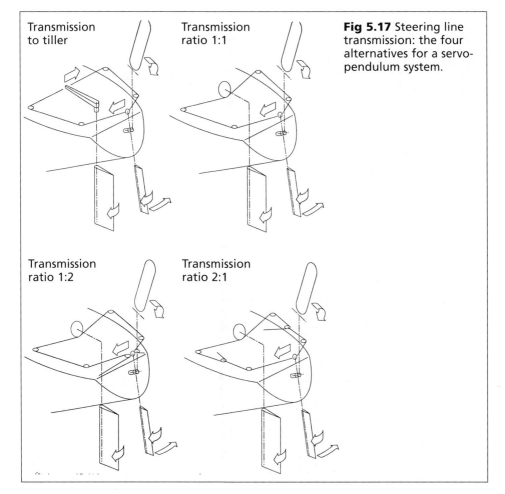

Transmission to tiller

Transmission ratio 1:1

Fig 5.17 Steering line transmission: the four alternatives for a servo-pendulum system.

Transmission ratio 1:2

Transmission ratio 2:1

generally go from lock to lock in fewer revolutions, so a wheel adaptor on a large diameter wheel has to exert more force with less line travel.

There are three main alternative arrangements for transmitting force from a servo-pendulum gear to a wheel steering system. The steering lines may be reeved as follows:

- Directly, ie 1:1
- Doubled up, ie double the line travel for half the force
- Running blocks, ie half the line travel for double the force

These systems all provide adequate steering performance if installed appropriately. Nevertheless, none

can touch the quality of transmission possible using a tiller with its adjustable attachment point and transmission ratio and much shorter transmission path. Windpilot has introduced an infinite transmission force adjustment facility on their Pacific model in 1998, giving it the same range of adjustment as a tiller.

Tip: Running both the steering lines to the wheel adaptor along the same side of the cockpit keeps access free on the other side. The four lines in the cockpit (two leading from the gear and two for connecting these to the wheel adaptor) can easily be mixed up in this configuration, so the

Steering lines led to one side; connection point with snap-shackles.

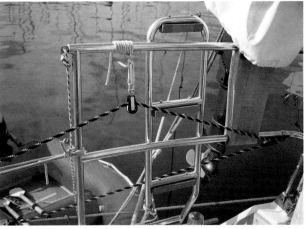

Steering lines can be tensioned easily using an additional block.

The Windpilot Pacific (1998 model) has an infinite transmission force facility.

pairs that belong together should be clearly marked. It may also be useful to fit four snap-shackles as connectors for joining the lines.

Slack and stretch are most easily cured by positioning an additional turning block on one of the lines between two existing blocks and moving it up, down or to one side to tension the steering lines. When the additional block is released, the slack returns and the connectors (snap-shackles) joining the gear to the wheel adaptor can be opened easily.

The factors highlighted as being detrimental to transmission efficiency with tiller steering also apply to wheel steering. Deficiencies in the boat's own steering system (eg stiff rudder, slack, poor transmission) can further reduce efficiency, so not all of the original 25 cm/10 in steering line travel (see Steering line travel, p 55) is ultimately available for turning the main rudder and steering the boat.

Setting the wheel adaptor

Most wheel adaptors conform to the same basic design. The various models do, however, differ substantially in their technical features, as we shall now explain:

1 *The fixed drum* No adjustment possible (Sailomat, Cap Horn). Both steering lines have to be disconnected from the adaptor and shortened/lengthened in order to fine-trim the course. This is not a straightforward procedure and fine-trim is often ignored, resulting in less efficient sailing. Providing sufficient scope for such adjustments also means that the lines have to be longer and additional turning blocks may be needed.

2 *Adjustable track adaptor* (Monitor). A spring-loaded pin engages in a hole in the circular track to hold

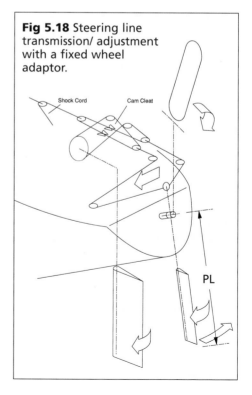

Fig 5.18 Steering line transmission/ adjustment with a fixed wheel adaptor.

Shock Cord   Cam Cleat

PL

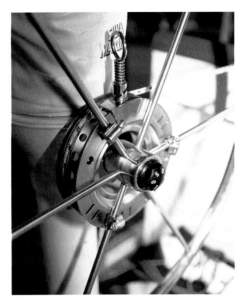

the drum in the desired position. Fine-trim involves pulling out the pin and rotating the drum until the pin aligns with a hole in the new desired position.

3 *Gearwheel adaptor* (Aries). The adaptor is mounted via a finely toothed gearwheel and is engaged/disengaged using a clutch. It must first be disengaged for fine-trimming.

4 *Disc brake style infinitely adjustable adaptor* (Windpilot Pacific). The adaptor is mounted via a disc on which it can be rotated and then fixed in place with a locking brake. The locking brake should be tightened no more than necessary to hold the adaptor in place. The adaptor is then able to slip on the disc when overloaded, for example in a sudden squall, preventing damage to the transmission components. This type of adaptor is very simple to adjust, with a little slack in the locking brake while the wheel is repositioned being all that is required.

The mounting diameter of a wheel adaptor may be a problem if it clashes with the mounting diameter of an autopilot already present.

Three wheel adaptors (top to bottom): Monitor, Aries and Windpilot.

Three wheel adaptors (left to right): Aries, Monitor and Windpilot.

Transmission to an emergency tiller
It is possible with almost all wheel-steering boats to fit an emergency tiller to ensure steering should the wheel system fail. Do not be tempted to try and improve the transmission efficiency of your system by simply connecting it to the emergency tiller! It will not work because the tiller will also be trying to turn the whole steering mechanism from the wrong end. The effect resembles trying to turn the steering wheel of a car by sitting in the road tugging on the front wheels.

The benefits of tiller steering can only be had by completely disconnecting the wheel-steering mechanism from the rudder quadrant. While impractical for weekend and holiday sailing, this is a perfectly realistic proposition for blue water yachts. The windvane gear handles most of the helming duties on a longer trip anyway, so losing the use of the wheel may be a small price to pay for the advantages of direct transmission to the tiller. This solution is only expedient if the following conditions are met:

1   The emergency tiller must be long enough for manual steering.
2   The emergency tiller must be within easy reach of the helmsperson; under no circumstances may it be outside the cockpit on the afterdeck.
3   The emergency tiller must be tightly clamped to the rudder post and there should be no play in the connection.

If you are planning a new boat, good emergency rudder transmission can be built into the design (see Building a new boat, p 84).

Transmission to hydraulic wheel steering

Hydraulic steering systems are installed on boats where the rudder pressure is too high for a mechanical system or where, for convenience, the boat can be helmed from more than one steering position. Steering force transmission through a system of hydraulic pumps and cylinders is always indirect. The wheel takes considerably more turns to go from lock to lock than with a mechanical system, and this is one reason why servo-pendulum gears are not really practical on boats with hydraulic steering. The second reason is that there is a degree of slippage in most hydraulic systems, caused by oil leaking out around bad seals (eg around packing rings). A servo-pendulum gear requires the rudder amidships position of the wheel always to be the same, which is seldom the case with hydraulic steering.

Transmission to an emergency tiller
This tempting alternative is only workable if the whole hydraulic system, including the main hydraulic cylinder, has been disconnected from the quadrant. Unless this is done, the emergency tiller will be trying to operate the steering hydraulics in reverse (as discussed under mechanical wheel steering).

The main source of resistance in the steering system is always the main hydraulic cylinder, so installing a bypass valve will solve nothing. In the end, it is better just to disconnect the hydraulics and give the servo-pendulum gear a chance to steer properly than to spend the voyage steering by hand or experimenting with other approaches.

Overload protection

In the transmission components

The steering lines of a servo-pendulum gear should always be pre-stressed rope and should have a diameter of at least 6 mm/$\frac{1}{4}$ in or, better still, 8 mm/$\frac{1}{3}$ in. Lines of this nature have breaking strains well above the maximum steering forces (300 kg/660 lb) that they are likely to meet so they will stretch little in use.

If the rudder suddenly loses control or the boat is hit by a gust, a servo-pendulum gear will exert its full force on the steering lines and the main rudder. The force in the steering lines can be enough to bend the stanchions or pushpit to which the steering line turning blocks are bolted. A good safety measure in this respect is to make sure that one block on each side of the boat is fastened to the rail with just a cord lanyard, which will break if overloaded and thus protect everything else.

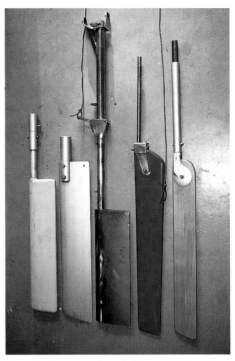

Overload protection (left to right): Aries, Sailomat, Monitor, Windpilot Pacific (old), Windpilot Pacific (new).

In the rudder shaft

The rudder blade of a servo-pendulum gear trailing along in the water could hardly be better for catching kelp, fishing nets and general flotsam, and overload protection should therefore be regarded as a priority. Here are the options:

1 A designated emergency breaking point between the rudder shaft and the pendulum arm is incorporated in the form of a notched tube (Aries). The breaking parameters are difficult to determine: the total leverage exerted by the rudder can be quite large, so it is hard to know at what stage the breaking point will give way and at what stage the whole gear will rip out of its mountings. The pendulum rudder should be tied to the mounting

with a safety line so that it is not lost when the shaft breaks.

2 The connection between the rudder blade and the shaft is protected by a spring-loaded catch which releases if the blade strikes anything (Monitor). This design effectively protects both the rudder blade and the mounting against collision damage.

3 The rudder blade is held in the forked end of the shaft by a rubber band (Cap Horn) or splint (Atoms) which gives when the rudder blade is overloaded.

4 The rudder blade is kept from pivoting up by lateral M8 Delrin bolts (Sailomat 601). The force required to shear an M8 bolt is often too large in practice to prevent damage to the gear mounting.

The Windpilot Pacific cuts smoothly through the water causing little drag.

5 The rudder blade is retained in a large area shaft fork by friction. As long as the bolt that closes the fork is not overtightened, the rudder can pivot up fore-or-aft in a collision (Windpilot Pacific). The rudder blade in this design must be positioned carefully to ensure that it is balanced. Subtle changes in the balance increase or decrease the sensitivity of the gear.

Tip: The rudder blade of a servo-pendulum system should not be fully immersed until the boat speed is approaching hull speed – that is, until the system needs to generate maximum force. This means that when the boat is stationary, the top of the rudder blade will be a certain distance out of the water. The stern wave on some boats, especially those with more traditional sterns, can rise surprisingly

high above the level of the surrounding water, so the exact distance will depend on the type of boat. If the rudder blade is too deeply immersed, the shaft will drag through the water, causing unnecessary turbulence and slowing the boat. This is easily avoided by mounting the system higher on the transom, which also improves the operation of the windvane.

The pendulum rudder: material, buoyancy, shape and balance

A pendulum rudder should react as sensitively as possible to every steering signal from the windvane. A balanced shaft design and buoyancy in the rudder blade improve the sensitivity of the gear, and the shaft and rudder blade should ideally be no heavier than absolutely necessary. The loads on a pendulum rudder and its shaft are for the most part only moderate; even pounding through waves is unlikely to damage the gear in its protected position at the stern. Nevertheless, the force generated by the pendulum rudder does make significant demands on the axle on which the pendulum arm swings. This is reflected in the visibly stronger construction employed in modern systems (Sailomat 601, Windpilot Pacific). For technical comparison see the table on p 64.

The pendulum rudder does not need to have a perfect profiled section because its maximum angle of attack is inherently very small. Every time the windvane rotates the rudder blade and increases the angle of attack, the blade swings out to one side and immediately reduces the angle back to approximately zero. The angle of attack, which is a function of the rudder pressure

Technical comparison

	Aries Std	Monitor	Sailomat 601	Windpilot Pacific
Pendulum arm axle diameter	25 mm/1 in	19 mm/$\frac{3}{4}$ in	40 mm/1$\frac{1}{2}$ in	44 mm/1$\frac{3}{4}$ in
Rudder shaft tube dimensions	38 x 6.5 mm/ 1$\frac{1}{2}$ x $\frac{1}{4}$ in	41.3 x 1.25 mm/ 1$\frac{1}{16}$ x $\frac{1}{20}$ in	50 x 4 mm/ 2 x $\frac{1}{6}$ in	40 x 5 mm/ 1$\frac{1}{2}$ x $\frac{1}{5}$ in
Rudder profile section	170 x 50 mm/ 6$\frac{3}{4}$ x 2 in	205 x 46 mm/ 8 x 1$\frac{3}{4}$ in	170 x 25mm/ 6$\frac{3}{4}$ x 1 in	120 x 19 mm/ 4$\frac{3}{4}$ x $\frac{3}{4}$ in
Rudder area	0.130 m^2	0.125 m^2	0.162 m^2	0.110 m^2
Rudder balance proportion	19.4%	19.5%	20.6%	22.5%
Rudder material	glassfibre foam	stainless/ foam	aluminium	wood epoxy
Buoyant	yes	yes	no	yes

required (to bring the boat back on course), never exceeds 3–5°. Such small figures effectively preclude flow separation, and the truth of the matter is that in an emergency even a simple wooden slat can function as a pendulum rudder blade, assuming it can be fastened to the shaft (no problem with the forked shaft of the Sailomat 601 or Windpilot Pacific).

The balance proportions of the pendulum rudder directly influence the sensitivity of the whole system. If the gear is to deliver good steering performance in light air, for instance, even a relatively weak steering signal should suffice to effect a sustained deflection or rotation of the pendulum rudder. A pendulum rudder with a large or variable balance propor-tion is inherently easier to rotate than one that is completely unbalanced.

Ultimately, steering performance is determined by the combined effect of all the various parameters involved in the functioning of the windvane steering system. Refining each parameter in turn takes consid-erable practical experience and test-ing, so it is unsurprising that the major manufacturers all go their own way in this respect.

The rudder profiles (depth and width of section) and balance propor-tions of the most common servo-pen-dulum systems are shown in the table above.

Setting the windvane to the wind direction

V vane

The setting procedure is the same as for an auxiliary rudder gear with a V vane. The windvane can be isolated completely from the system so that it swings freely in the wind totally independently of the steering. Once set and connected, the gear can be fine-trimmed using an endless worm gear. The V vane can be moved in or out on its mounting to compensate for different wind strengths in the same way as with an auxiliary rud-der system.

H vane

There are four alternative approaches

1 *Manual* The locking device is released, the vane support is positioned by hand and the locking device is then tightened again (Sailomat). This method involves a crew member working right at the stern, which may be unpleasant or even dangerous at night. There is no scale to indicate the position of the vane relative to the wind.

2 *Toothed wheel and chain* The vane is positioned using a toothed wheel and chain arrangement similar to that on a bicycle. This method allows infinite adjustment and can be adapted to allow remote control (Monitor). Again no scale is provided.

3 *6° increment toothed wheel and latch* The vane is adjusted by rotating a toothed wheel into the correct position before engaging a latch (Aries). The wheel turns in increments of 6°, which is often far too coarse going to weather, and the whole arrangement is heavy and fiddly to use.

4 *Worm gear* The vane support is positioned using an endless worm gear (Windpilot Pacific). This system is easy to operate and lends itself to remote control. An additional advantage of a worm gear is that it can be fitted with a scale to show the angle of the vane to the wind, making it easier to set the course.

The vane can be adjusted for different wind strengths as explained in the H vane section. Remote control is handy not only for convenience but also for safety – nobody enjoys dangling off the back of the boat in the middle of the night trying to make course adjustments.

Ease of installation

Installing a conventional servo-pendulum gear is a substantial project. The major complication is that, as transom designs are so different, most

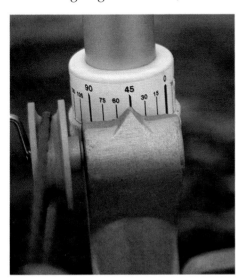

The infinite remote control, with its scale in degrees, is easy to read on the Windpilot Pacific.

Conventional servo-pendulum systems often require the mounting components to be customised.

Servo-pendulum systems with a vertical pendulum arm may need extended mounting brackets on modern forward -raked transoms.

In the raised position, the pendulum rudder of the Windpilot does not stick out beyond the stern because of its angled shaft.

boats will need the mounting components to be tailor-made – something of a headache for the DIY skipper. Faced with an outboard rudder or extreme sugar-scoop stern, the classic mounting arrangement of a traditional Aries has little to offer. An elaborate and heavy tubular construction is the only solution, although the actual forces acting on a servo-pendulum gear transom bracket are surprisingly small (as we shall discuss later on).

Modern systems come with a variable mounting flange which can be adjusted to fit a wide range of transom angles without any special adaptor, rendering installation much more straightforward. It should be borne in mind in respect of boats with a forward-raked transom that most servo-pendulum gears only function properly with the pendulum arm vertical; the system may have to overhang aft

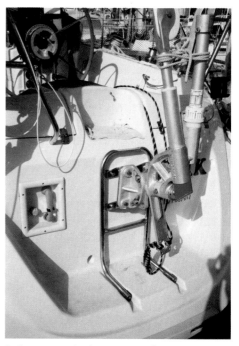

Release one bolt, remove the system and the swim ladder is ready for use.

by some distance to ensure that the rudder shaft clears the bottom edge of the transom.

The overhang, of course, adds further to the weight of the gear. Almost all servo-pendulum systems have vertical pendulum arms. The only exceptions are Windpilot Pacific and Sailomat, on which the pendulum rudder axis is angled aft by 10° and 34° respectively. The significance of this for forward sloping transoms (by far the most common design) is that even with the system mounted close against the transom, the pendulum rudder shaft will still clear the bottom or aft edge. Mounting the system right up against the transom also means that when the pendulum rudder is pivoted up out of the water, it no longer sticks out beyond the aft edge of the transom. This is a considerable advantage for manoeuvring in tight harbours or landing stern first in the Mediterranean, as no part of the gear sticks out beyond the outline of the boat.

Installation position

It almost goes without saying that the only place for a servo-pendulum gear is the centre of the transom. Symmetrical mounting is essential for smooth operation, and offset mounting, for example to avoid a swim ladder, never yields satisfactory results. All boats generate slight weather helm as a function of design, so windvane gears are almost always called upon to turn the boat away from the wind. The inherent geometry of a servo-pendulum gear dictates that the pendulum swings out to weather – that is, towards the high side – in order to bear away. If the system is mounted to one side the pendulum arm ends up much further

out of the water when that side is the high side and will come right out of the water during a big course deviation. Extending the pendulum arm merely transfers the problem to the other tack, when the rudder shaft will be submerged along with its blade, creating more drag.

The big misconception

Servo-pendulum systems operate on the basis of servo-dynamic force. Essentially, the mounting at the stern only has to withstand the force transmitted through the steering lines to the main rudder and support the gear itself. High loads, such as pounding waves, do not as a rule reach the gear, and breaking waves are more likely to knock the whole boat to leeward than force the pendulum rudder out of its position in the wake. A swell that catches the boat side-on acts on

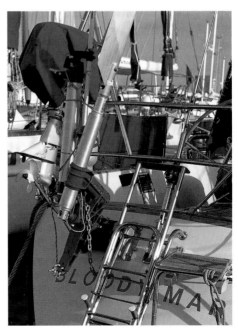

An offset mounted servo-pendulum system will not function effectively.

This mounting for a Windpilot Pacific on a 25 tonne gaff cutter has worked well for 12 years.

not only the pendulum rudder but also the main rudder, causing both to rotate slightly and absorb some of the force of the wave. The connecting lines from the gear to the main rudder thus act as a kind of sliding clutch, allowing the steering system as a whole to damp every movement.

Notice how the Pacific gear is fastened (four bolts) to the heavy gaff cutter shown in the photograph (left). Despite its fragile appearance, the mounting already has 12 trouble-free years of service behind it, including plenty of blue water mileage. This should not really seem so surprising: the pendulum rudder follows the boat as effortlessly as a gull behind a trawler when the steering lines are disconnected, so the load on the mounting amounts to nothing more than the weight of the gear. Reconnecting the steering lines adds only the force generated by the pendulum rudder to turn the main rudder and effect the course correction.

Mounting on a 20 tonne Colin Archer.

Mounting on a Helmsman 49.

Experience, of course, is the real test. If wave action really could bring damagingly large forces to bear on a trailing pendulum rudder blade and its mounting, we would expect to find at least a few instances amongst the thousands of Aries and Monitor systems in use of the pendulum arm being bent against the steering line guide tubes that extend at the bottom of both these systems. This type of damage turns out to be all but unheard of. The configuration of the bevel gear linkage in both systems ensures that the pendulum arm is always brought back into parallel with the keel (ie is damped) before it can travel so far sideways. This remains true regardless of wave action or even capsize.

Wooden, steel, aluminium and solid laminated GRP hulls need no extra reinforcement on the inside of the transom. Only on sandwich construction hulls is it recommended to fit additional wooden blocks or aluminium plates rather than sandwich material at load bearing points.

The apparently greater load distribution provided by the larger number of bolts (up to 16) on conventional servo-pendulum systems (Aries, Monitor) is not technically necessary, and the mass of bolts contributes to the visual pollution of the stern. The loads may simply have been overestimated by the designers at the time when these traditional servo-pendulum systems were conceived.

Ease of use

Removal
The ease with which a servo-pendulum gear can be removed seems fairly irrelevant for a blue water voyage. In other situations – for example, if a

protruding gear is likely to be hit or to prevent theft during winter storage – it is helpful if the system can be removed without too much trouble. With the Windpilot Pacific and Sailomat 600 models this can be accomplished by undoing just a single bolt. Most other systems are retained by several bolts.

Operation
A good servo-pendulum system should be simple to set up and, most importantly, should permit the user to raise the pendulum rudder up out of the water very quickly. Operation should be straightforward enough that a helmsperson will engage the system even for short absences from the helm – for example, during a quick trip to the nav-station. Along with their visual drawbacks, the difficulty of operating conventional servo-pendulum systems is probably the main reason why many sailors initially opt for an autopilot.

Rudder blade not in use, Monitor.

Rudder blade not in use, Atoms.

Rudder blade not in use, Fleming.

Rudder blade not in use, Aries Lift-Up.

Rudder blade not in use, Navik.

Rudder blade raised, Sailomat 601.

Rudder blade raised, Windpilot Pacific.

Space requirement of a Monitor.

Space requirement of a Windpilot Pacific.

A pendulum rudder cannot be prevented from moving around. Consequently, unless raised before motoring in reverse it will interrupt the manoeuvre as soon as the flow from astern is sufficient to deflect it.

Modern systems allow the pendulum rudder to be raised easily whenever necessary, the only proviso being that the boat must be slowed down enough to ensure the force of the water flowing by does not hold the pendulum arm in place. Conventional systems, in contrast, have a catch on the rudder which must be released before the pendulum rudder can be raised in the shaft fork or swung up to one side.

Dimensions and weight

Over the years the bulk and, sometimes, considerable weight of servo-pendulum systems have driven many potential buyers to look elsewhere. These handicaps have now been consigned to history: while a conventional servo-pendulum gear might once have weighed around 35 kg/77 lb, a modern system tips the scales at a mere 20 kg/44 lb – and is also a good deal stronger in the most important components.

Advantages and disadvantages

The outstanding feature of all servo-pendulum systems is their huge servo force, strong enough, given a good transmission arrangement, to steer boats of 18 m/60 ft and 30 tonnes. Under normal conditions, a servo-pendulum gear will be able to steer the boat as long as forward progress is being made and the flow past the hull is sufficient to push the pendulum rudder one way or the other. Servo-pendulum gears generate several times the force of a simple auxiliary rudder system.

One drawback of this type of gear is the care required to set up the steering lines properly. Poorly arranged steering lines reduce efficiency and can even disable the whole system. Because line travel is limited to 25 cm/10 in, longer transmission paths unavoidably impair steering performance. If the system keeps no line travel in reserve during normal operation, it is inevitable that the rudder will eventually lose control in demanding conditions. Transmission is always worse with wheel steering; the degree of deterioration depends on the characteristics of the system in question.

Practical steering force transmission to a centre-cockpit wheel is very difficult because the transmission paths are so long. The use of stainless steel wire offers some improvement here, but entails other problems (eg turning block wear).

There is no way of using a servo-pendulum gear for emergency steering: it is impossible to fix the pendulum arm in place, and in any case the rudder blade lacks sufficient area to provide acceptable steering in difficult conditions. A $0.1 \, m^2/1 \, ft^2$ pendulum rudder blade could not possibly be up to steering a boat in seas rough enough to break a main rudder. Servo-pendulum gears are not normally designed to handle the loads associated with emergency rudder use, so any system that is nevertheless recommended by its manufacturer for this purpose will need substantial structural reinforcement to stabilise the pendulum arm.

The Sailomat 601 has to be fixed in place using lines at the sides that are tied to the pushpit. The shaft and rudder are strengthened to ensure that the rudder does not break away when the lines are in place, but this reinforcement means the rudder and stock are heavier for self-steering operation.

The pendulum rudder on a Monitor gear can be replaced with a larger emergency rudder, the shaft then needing six lines for lateral stability.

V vane servo-pendulum systems: Hasler, Schwingpilot.

H vane servo-pendulum systems:
1 Bevel gear yaw damping: Aries, Fleming, Monitor, Windpilot Pacific.
2 Other forms of yaw damping: Cap Horn, Sailomat 601, Navik, Atoms.

Double rudder systems

How they work

A double rudder system combines the advantages of a powerful servo-pendulum system and an auxiliary rudder that is independent of the main rudder to give the best possible steering performance. The main rudder is fixed in place and used for fine-trimming the set course, leaving the double rudder gear to undertake course corrections free from any weather helm.

Steering impulse	=	wind
Steering force	=	water
Steering element	=	auxiliary rudder
Power leverage (PL)	=	up to 200 cm/ 80 in

System suitability

This type of system is particularly suitable in cases where:

1 The boat is too large or heavy to be managed by a simple auxiliary rudder;

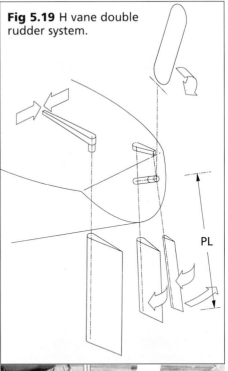

Fig 5.19 H vane double rudder system.

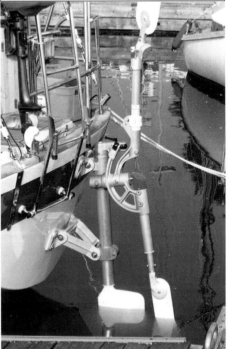

Windpilot Pacific Plus fitted on a Hallberg Rassy 36.

2 The transmission paths are too long for efficient use of a servo-pendulum gear (especially on boats with a centre cockpit);

3 The planned voyage is long, the crew small, and consequently the very best steering performance is sought;

4 The presence of an emergency rudder is considered to be important, for instance on boats where the main rudder is not protected by a skeg;

5 The boat has a hydraulic rudder system – double rudder systems are the only form of self-steering that can be used on such boats (see p 76 hydraulic wheel steering).

World-wide, only two double rudder systems have ever gone into series production:

Sailomat 3040

This unit was originally designed for boats between 30 and 40 feet long (hence the name 3040). An H vane passes the steering impulse to a pendulum rudder whose shaft is inclined by 30°. The shaft has an upper extension that is attached to the auxiliary rudder so as to exert a force in the opposite direction to the movement of the pendulum rudder blade. The inclination of the shaft provides yaw damping.

This gear was produced between 1976 and 1981 and features a particularly compact linkage housing, the top and bottom of which also serve as the bracket for mounting the gear on the transom. The small size of the bracket means that the loads from the gear are concentrated in a very small area. GRP boats consequently require large-scale reinforcement at the stern to support the high loads generated by the auxiliary rudder.

The fastening points of an auxiliary rudder system, and hence of a double rudder system, should ideally be spaced well apart to ensure good load distribution on the transom. The upper and lower regions of the transom naturally possess greater dimensional stability than the centre, so spacing the fastening points apart all but eliminates vibration as well.

The chief drawback of this particular system, aside from expense, is that it is rather complicated for everyday use. Removing the pendulum rudder involves releasing its fastening and then dropping it out of the bottom of its shaft – an awkward operation to perform every time you need to manoeuvre in harbour. The nature of the design restricts the lateral swinging range of the pendulum rudder arm to 20° in each direction. Any further than this and the top of

Sailomat 3040 fitted on a Hallberg Rassy 352.

the shaft hits its end stops in the gearbox. This can be a real problem in big seas: Naomi James worked her way through a good handful of replacement rudder blades in the course of her remarkable circumnavigation with *Express Crusader*.

Windpilot Pacific Plus

Windpilot's Pacific Plus has been around since 1986. It is probably the only double rudder system in the world to have been series-built during that period. The design reflects all the progress made over four decades of windvane steering development. The steering characteristics have been optimised and the system uses a bevel gear linkage for yaw damping and a horizontal windvane inclined by 20°. An endless worm gear provides remote operation. The pendulum rudder can be raised when the system is idle and the auxiliary rudder makes a good emergency rudder. The design aesthetics are modern and the modular construction makes installation of the system and removal of the pendulum components a simple task. The positioning of the auxiliary rudder right at the aft end of the boat also provides optimum leverage and, as a result, particularly effective steering.These are the effective auxiliary rudder areas.

Pacific Plus I $= 0.27 \, \mathrm{m}^2 / 2\frac{3}{4} \, \mathrm{ft}^2$
Pacific Plus II $= 0.36 \, \mathrm{m}^2 / 3\frac{2}{3} \, \mathrm{ft}^2$
Pacific Plus III $= 0.50 \, \mathrm{m}^2 / 5\frac{1}{2} \, \mathrm{ft}^2$

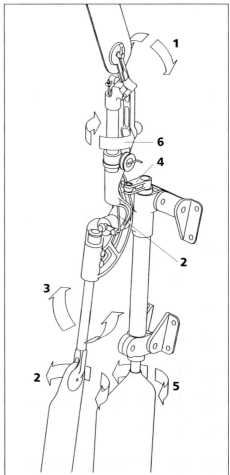

Fig 5.20 Windpilot Pacific Plus: **1** Windvane is deflected by wind and gives steering signal. **2** Via linkage, it turns the pendulum rudder. **3** Water flowing past pushes the pendulum arm out to one side; a linkage **(4)** connecting the pendulum arm to the auxiliary rudder **(5)** transmits the steering signal. **6** The vane mounting can be rotated through a full 360°.

The pendulum rudder sits immediately behind the auxiliary rudder. This means that the two elements can be connected directly, eliminating the transmission losses (due to slack, stretch or bearing friction) typical of servo-pendulum systems, where the steering force reaches the main rudder via lines. This linkage between the gear's two rudders originally comprised a novel ball-and-socket joint. Once the ball socket in the tiller part of the auxiliary rudder had been loosened, the connection could be released, allowing the pendulum arm to be swung up out of the water. The pendulum rudder on the equivalent Sailomat unit, which lacked this feature, could only be removed by dropping it out of the bottom of the system.

Starting with the 1998 model, the Pacific Plus now has a bevel gear rocker segment connection between the pendulum and auxiliary rudder. This 'Quick-in, Quick-out' linkage can be released with one hand even under load. A special device ensures that the auxiliary rudder remains centred when it is out of use and the pendulum rudder is in the raised position. The Pacific Plus also has a facility which allows the windvane to be fixed on centre. Engaging this feature prevents the pendulum rudder from starting to swing around as soon as it is lowered into the water. Once the bevel gear linkage has been reconnected, the windvane is released and the system begins to work. A retaining pin for connecting up a tiller autopilot is also standard on the current model.

Use with hydraulic steering

Double rudder systems only function properly with hydraulic wheel steering if the flow of fluid in the hydraulic system can be completely and reliably blocked. Any leakage, however slight, makes the main rudder susceptible to deflection by wave action or water pressure and therefore renders it useless for fine-trimming the course and countering weather helm. Double rudder gears rely on the lateral surface area of the main rudder; they can only steer the boat as long as the main rudder stays in its set position.

Hydraulic systems sometimes incur damage and develop leaks while underway. The only solution if this happens on an extended voyage is to fit the emergency tiller and then lash it in place with lines, either above or below deck, to hold the main rudder in place.

Fields of use

Double rudder systems are used mainly in blue water sailing since this

Above right and left: The 1998 Pacific Plus has 'Quick-in, Quick-out' linkage between the pendulum and auxiliary rudders.

A typical centre-cockpit cruising boat, a Danish Motiva 41, sailing round the world.

is the arena in which their excellent steering qualities are especially telling. They are also particularly well suited to the centre-cockpit designs increasingly favoured by yacht manufacturers such as Hallberg Rassy, Oyster, Westerly, Moody, Najad, Malö, Camper & Nicholson and Amel. The auxiliary rudder is something of a handicap when manoeuvring in harbour, which reduces the appeal of this type of gear for weekend and holiday sailors.

For a small crew on a long trip, though, the steering performance of a windvane steering system can never be too good. Inadequate steering, regardless of the cause (poor choice of system, transmission problems in a servo-pendulum system), always manifests itself in difficult wind and sea conditions when manual steering is at its most unpleasant. Double rudder systems represent the very best in windvane steering force and performance. They combine the advantages

of auxiliary rudders and servo-pendulum gears (with none of the attendant transmission problems): the connection between the pendulum rudder and its dedicated auxiliary rudder is direct, and the auxiliary rudder, relieved by the main rudder of any basic steering functions, effects course corrections with maximum leverage thanks to its position at the very aft end of the boat.

A theory surfaces from time to time which suggests that a pendulum rudder should provide better steering through a boat's main rudder because the main rudder has a far greater area than any auxiliary rudder. This reflects a misunderstanding of the interactions between the elements involved in steering. The main rudder is designed to cope with all potential steering tasks under sail or engine where sudden course changes (eg tacking) require a large rudder angle setting while the rudder angles required for course corrections, though, are always small. In any case, the relatively short line travel and ever-present transmission losses (weather helm, stretch, slack, play, wheel steering and its transmission to the main rudder quadrant, friction in the main rudder bearings) restrict the amount by which the pendulum rudder can turn the main rudder.

The ultimate limits of windvane steering

When there is no wind there can be no steering signal, but a sensitive windvane system will start to function as soon as there is enough wind to fill the sails and set the boat moving.

A servo-pendulum gear needs about 2 knots of speed through the water before the water flowing past the hull can generate the force required in the pendulum rudder blade and steering lines to turn the main rudder. Unfortunately, this all presupposes a calm sea. If the sails are collapsed by left-over swells, the boat will lose its drive and the windvane system will have nothing left to offer. The only remedy here is an autopilot.

Stronger winds generate a stronger steering impulse from the windvane and improved boat speed increases the force available from the pendulum rudder. If the boat is perfectly trimmed – that is, the steering force required is low – the pendulum rudder will swing out just a small distance and exert only moderate force on the main rudder. Not until the boat requires greater rudder pressure does the system bring its full reserves of power into play. To meet the need for more force, the pendulum rudder swings out further from the centreline – thereby increasing its leverage and generating considerably more steering force. This illustrates how proper and effective

ULDB *Budapest* just after launching in Slovenia, June 1996.

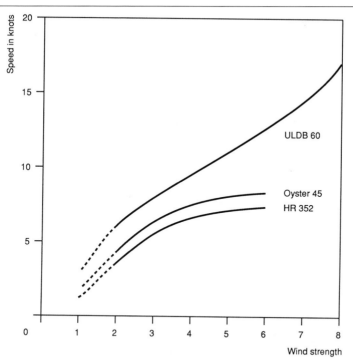

Fig 5.21 This figure uses the same formula as Fig 5.14 but here it is boat speed rather than torque which is plotted against wind strength.

The pendulum rudder rotation angle assumed here, 6°, is intentionally on the high side in order to illustrate the tensile forces theoretically possible. Rotation angles of 0–3° are more realistic as the tensile forces required at the main rudder of a properly trimmed boat are very much lower. In principle, the poorer the trim, the higher the tensile forces that will be required at the main rudder; thus the greater the rotation angle needed at the pendulum rudder before the feedback from the windvane signals a return to the desired course and the pendulum rudder/pendulum arm is restored to centre. This automatically entails a larger yawing angle. The faster the system reacts, the smoother the course will be.

For boats whose maximum speed is limited by design as a function of length along the waterline, the curve plotted in the figure ends when the boat reaches hull speed.

For boats whose maximum speed is much higher or even unlimited (ULDBs, catamarans), the curve continues appropriately. A windvane steering system has to give up going to weather if the acceleration of the boat when accidentally bearing away (rudder or swells) is so great that it pushes the apparent wind angle forward to the point where the windvane can no longer tell what is happening; the apparent wind angle on the faster and lower course is exactly the same as that on the original slower, higher course. What generally happens is that the boat falls some way off the wind, accelerating sharply, and the windvane detects no difference and institutes no corrective rudder movement (see The ultimate limits of windvane steering systems).

Remember: Windvane steering systems cannot be trusted to manage planing boats, since the principles outlined above preclude a reliable steering impulse. The danger of a crash-gybe is ever-present once the windvane becomes confused; only the most irresponsible skipper would risk losing the mast just to save some time at the helm.

damping gives servo-pendulum gears such an advantage in terms of range of conditions and power reserves: steering quality generally increases as wind strength and boat speed increase.

This trend holds until breaking seas make manual steering compulsory. A windvane steering system cannot see breaking waves and just carries on steering right through them, a potentially dangerous habit for both vessel and crew. Blind South African sailor, Geoffrey Hilton Barber who crossed the Indian Ocean from Durban to Freemantle in seven weeks in 1997, even trusted his Windpilot Pacific in a 65 knot gale under bare poles.

Ocean racing

Experience with ultralight displacement boats (ULDBs) of all sizes has shown that the speed potential of these flyers is just too great to be effectively entrusted to windvane steering. Every change in wind speed aboard such responsive boats produces a change in boat speed which, in turn, changes the apparent wind angle. The acceleration and deceleration of the boat through puffs and lulls causes the apparent wind angle to move forward or aft. A windvane gear steering to a particular set wind angle would, as a result, have to head up or bear away every time the wind speed changed in order to maintain the set angle.

Most monohulls, and virtually all cruising boats, are limited in terms of speed as a function of their length along the waterline and do not accelerate fast enough to provoke significant changes in the apparent wind

angle. Monohull ULDBs have no such restrictions on speed. Bow, hull shape, keel, displacement and sail area are all conceived to promote surfing even in fairly moderate winds; the design encourages tremendous acceleration, inevitably accompanied by tremendous fluctuations in the apparent wind angle.

This type of sailing is quite simply beyond the capabilities of any windvane gear. The kind of wild course produced by any system relying purely on the apparent wind angle would bring the rig down sooner or later – for example, in a sudden crash gybe. Things do not necessarily look any brighter on upwind courses. Even with the sails close-hauled, the smallest deviation to leeward (in a swell or a yawing movement) causes the boat to accelerate rapidly, in turn pushing the apparent wind forward. A windvane has no way of telling whether the boat is travelling slower on a very high course or faster on a deeper course, because the apparent wind angle is identical in both cases. This really does represent the end of the line for windvane steering, since there is no way of educating a windvane to distinguish between different situations that generate the same physical effects. Autopilots offer the only effective solution here.

Off the wind, and to some extent even upwind, planing yachts are beyond the scope of windvane steering. *Cruising World* agreed in its 9/95 edition regarding the use of windvane steering systems in the BOC that, '...the current boats accelerate and decelerate at such extreme rates that windvane steering gears appear on few and conservative boats only'.

· 6 ·
Choosing a system

Materials

The materials used to manufacture windvane steering systems are normally determined by their production method. Most hand-made systems are fabricated from stainless steel. Aesthetics tend to be subordinate here to functionality, and such systems bear much of the blame for the reluctance of many sailors to (dis)grace their beautiful transom with a windvane steering system.

Another consideration is accuracy of construction. Hand-made systems are almost always built within certain tolerances; tubes bend, for example, when they are welded. The counter-argument to this, that tubular stainless steel models are easier to repair, fails to stand up in practice: few boats will carry the tools necessary to straighten a collision-damaged system.

Industrially produced systems are generally constructed in aluminium. The use of sand or die casting and CNC machine tools permits very precise manufacture of identically dimensioned components. This method of manufacture also gives the designer considerably more freedom to consider appearance.

Aluminium is not just aluminium. The majority of aluminium windvane steering systems are built in AlMg 3 grade alloy, although AlMg 5, which is completely resistant to salt water, is better. Aluminium ships, for example, are built in AlMg 4.5 grade alloy, a material which is able to resist the action of seawater even if left uncoated. Windvane gear components are either coated (Sailomat) or anodised (Hydrovane, Aries, Windpilot Pacific) for surface protection. Windpilot would appear to be the only manufacturer using high-grade AlMg 5 as standard.

Bearings

Ball, needle and self-aligning bearings are suitable for use in heavily loaded environments such as winches, genoa car blocks, rig and main rudder mounting. The loads involved in transmitting a steering impulse from the windvane to the linkage are tiny, so mountings here can be quite simple. The bearings mentioned can be used for the main bearing and the pendulum axle bearing, but fitting a shaft seal to protect them against ingress of salt water or crystals impairs their smooth running. Unprotected ball bearings begin to seize as salt crystals accumulate and require a degree of maintenance to keep them running smoothly.

This series of photographs shows the manufacturing procedure for sand-cast aluminium
a) Model and core of the Pacific Light in wood
b) Model assembly on the moulding plate
c) Model impression in sand with cores inserted
d) Removing the sand mould
e) The result

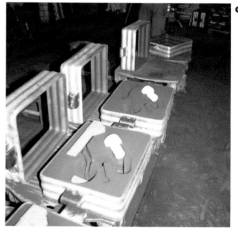

Anybody who has ever been driven by curiosity or boredom to take a windvane gear apart will surely have been shocked at the amount of dirt from the air and water which manages to accumulate in the bearings even in just one year. Salt crystals are easily removed at sea just by pouring on a little fresh water, but if your boat has spent a while moored downwind of a large town or city, you can expect to find much more troublesome deposits of oily harbour water in the bearings. Stripping down a bearing, as anybody who has tried it will confirm, takes steady hands and strong nerves – as well as a good memory to ensure there are as many ball bearings at the end as there were at the beginning!

Sliding bearings, made from PE, POM, DELRIN or PTFE Teflon, achieve their good sliding properties by absorbing a certain amount of moisture (air/water) and tend to be slightly larger. The sliding properties are barely affected by accumulated salt crystals or dirt in the bearing. Sliding bearings are more reliable and durable in long-term service and are easier to replace.

Maintenance

The times when maintenance for traditional Aries systems meant regularly oiling the sites marked with a dab of red paint are gone for good; no sailor today would put up with it. Windvane gears are robust, durable and very easily satisfied. Wear is absolutely minimal and, assuming they avoid any close encounters with the harbour wall, many systems can soldier on for 30 years or more. Windpilot systems often come back after a circumnavigation showing

hardly a trace of wear, even after one or two knock-downs on the way.

The minimum acceptable in terms of maintenance amounts to cleaning the bearings and checking all the bolts and screws. The windvane and rudder blade will also need recoating from time to time.

A word of caution: Oiling or greasing sliding bearings can lead to problems caused by gumming or chemical reaction with salt water, cancelling the good sliding properties. There are still some sailors who refuse to concede that grease, Vaseline® and silicone spray have no business getting into a sliding bearing, and are then surprised when their gear starts to stiffen up.

Tip: Fittings in the rig and on the spars, indeed screw connections of any type, will remain unseized for years if coated with lanolin. Lanolin, or wool wax, is the substance that keeps a sheep's fleece waterproof in the rain. Every boat should have a pot of lanolin on board – it also makes great hand cream! Another way of inhibiting any kind of electrolytic corrosion between different materials is to coat the contact area with Duralac jointing compound.

DIY construction

Twenty years ago the subject of homemade windvane steering systems merited a whole chapter in books like this one. But also, of course, twenty years ago the average boat in need of windvane steering was small enough to make DIY projects a practical alternative. The average length of today's blue water yachts is approaching 12 m/40 ft, and even much larger yachts are not uncommon. Most owners have considerably better financial resources now as well, so with the general standard of fitting out being so high, the home-made option seems less attractive.

The Bibliography lists older books on the subject of building your own windvane gear for any sailors of more moderate means who might still like to save some money this way. You should be aware, though, that there is a thriving second-hand market for good windvane systems for smaller boats. Older systems that are no longer in production have been included in the market summary in Chapter 11 to help with second-hand purchases.

We can only advise you, in the strongest possible terms, to ensure when planning a long trip on a small boat that you choose a capable and proven system rather than relying on a home-made system that falters when things get rough. Never lose sight of the bottom line: if your gear fails, you either steer by hand or go home early.

Building a new boat

When surveying the considerable number of new boats, both production models and one-offs, built for long-distance sailing, it is apparent that many errors are made with respect to self-steering equipment. When buying a brand name production yacht, many sailors simply rely on the competence of the broker. The boat then arrives with a whole host of complex electrical and electronic systems and only later does the owner discover how important (or unimportant) individual items are. Indeed there are even a few larger boatbuilders who simply refuse to install

windvane systems or offer offset swim ladders as a build option on their blue water yachts because this disrupts production. There is also perhaps an assumption here that somebody in the process of buying a new boat will be too preoccupied with other things to get around to requesting relocation of the swim ladder, even though it would create very little extra work for the builders. Of the huge number of Hallberg Rassy yachts currently steered by Windpilot, fewer than five had the gear fitted during production!

Sailors do, however, seem to be increasingly aware when buying a new boat that the ideal solution to all self-steering problems is a well-matched autopilot and windvane steering gear, a subject we shall return to in Chapter 7.

If you plan your self-steering requirements carefully, it is worth considering fitting a relatively small autopilot for operating the main rudder in addition to a windvane gear. Each system will then be in a position to cover different wind and sea conditions and the total expense will be lower. Boatbuilders usually install powerful autopilots, but these may well be inappropriate alongside a windvane gear because the autopilot will be used predominantly in calms and for motoring.

An important design consideration, when building a one-off for long-distance sailing, is the fact that once at sea steering will belong almost exclusively to the 'iron helm'. The operating characteristics of the planned self-steering equipment – for example, a windvane gear – should therefore be reflected in the design: tiller steering is always best for a servo-pendulum system (see

Self-steering gear is standard on these yachts moored at Las Palmas, November 1995.

Transmission to tiller steering, p 55). Even large, heavy ships can be designed with tiller steering if required. Some sailors will still prefer wheel steering, either as a matter of personal taste or because they are planning a centre cockpit. The inherent inferiority of wheel steering with regard to force transmission from servo-pendulum gears can easily be overcome by routing the steering through the emergency tiller. Many French wheel-steering boats feature an arrangement in which the force from the wheel is passed directly to the emergency tiller via lines rather than passing through the deck to a quadrant: free the tiller of the lines running from the wheel and it is ready for connection to a servo-pendulum gear. This makes an expensive double rudder system unnecessary.

Not only does tiller steering outshine wheel steering in terms of reliability and simplicity, it also indicates errors in trim or balance (eg the need to reef) much more clearly. The tiller strains visibly when weather helm is excessive.

Sometimes a hydraulic rudder system is essential for design reasons – for instance, if the boat has more than one steering position. Servo-pendulum rudders are only compatible with hydraulic steering given certain preconditions (see Hydraulic wheel-steering systems, p 61), so it is usually necessary to go with an auxiliary rudder or double rudder system. A reliable means of blocking the hydraulic system and keeping the main rudder stationary is absolutely critical here; if the main rudder is subject to the influences of wave action, the windvane gear will be functionally useless. It may eventually be necessary to physically fix the main rudder in place using the emergency tiller, which makes operation laborious because the emergency tiller has to be released every time the main rudder trim is altered.

The main rudder should ideally be well balanced. This keeps the required steering force low, enhancing the sensitivity of a windvane steering system and saving power with an autopilot.

The deck layout aft should reflect the fact that a windvane works better upwind the less turbulence it encounters. Seats, liferafts, dodgers on the lifelines, high cabin tops close to the stern, etc reduce the sensitivity of a windvane. Spray hoods and other projecting structures further away from the stern cause no such problems since no boat sails much closer than about 35° to the wind, and from the windvane this angle encloses nothing but open sea.

The bolts supporting a windvane steering system should always be accessible from the inside of the boat. Care must be taken not to obscure them when working down below at the stern – for example, when fitting out an aft cabin. If you are fitting a system on a finished boat and the aft cabin has wooden panelling, the best advice is to drill the bolt holes right through the hull and panelling from the outside and then cut away the wood around the bolt holes from the inside using a circle cutter. Once the system has been mounted the holes can be covered with wood, leaving the bolts concealed but still readily accessible.

The desired transom form is also of key importance when building a new boat. Modern transoms with an integrated swim platform (sugar scoop) are ideal for the installation of windvane steering systems as long as the platform does not extend too far aft, as this entails extra mounting work. Double rudder systems may even be installed with the auxiliary rudder part protected within the platform, either by inserting the shaft of the auxiliary rudder through the platform or, better still, by integrating a slot into the back of the platform. The pendulum rudder part in any case remains clear of the swim platform and can easily be swung up out of the water.

Another consideration for owners eyeing up the aft cabin as the owner's cabin: autopilot drive units operating on the rudder quadrant directly under the berth can be quite noisy and have been known to drive sailors out of their bunks. Mechanical linear drive units are much noisier than hydraulic linear drives.

Too many sailors wait until the very last minute before deciding to fit a windvane steering system. By this time, with departure imminent, the stern is already fully loaded and the ensuing tide of compromises required to find space for the vane gear causes sleepless nights for both owner and manufacturer. The fault does not always lie with the owner, however. Some boats have particular features which necessitate extra mounting work and additional (heavy) supporting structures. Worst of all are those with a platform at deck level whose design all but precludes the installation of a windvane gear. Often the only solution is a set of additional heavy mounting brackets below the platform, a proposition which tends to send owners into shock. The moral of the story is: lack of foresight with regard to the layout of the aft end of the boat is very difficult to rectify later on and the requisite compromises have a tendency towards the aesthetically offensive.

Above Sugar scoop of a Carena 40 fitted with a Windpilot Pacific Plus ready for an Atlantic crossing in November 1996.

Left Sugar scoop of a Taswell 48 showing a Windpilot Pacific Plus system with the pendulum arm in the raised position.

Types of boat

Choosing a boat can be anxious work. There are many pitfalls and potential mistakes that can be made, which only become apparent later, out at sea or in specific circumstances (eg bad weather). The following brief discussion of the basic types of boat should help to anticipate some of these pitfalls.

Long-keel boats

This classic form dominated yacht building for many years. The long keel promised good course-holding abilities and great seaworthiness, and provided a sound structural backbone for any yacht. The rudder hung at the aft end of the keel. S frame construction combined with V shaped frames in the whole bow section ensured smooth passage through the water and a calm and comfortable boat.

The courageous rescue missions of Norwegian sailor Colin Archer, who took his unmotorised double-ended cutter out into the North Atlantic to rescue imperilled fishermen even in hurricane force winds, live on in legend around the globe. His experiences spawned innumerable new designs and are synonymous with virtually unlimited seaworthiness. The CA mark is familiar to sailors the world over.

Bernard Moitessier was also a fan of the long keel, and selected one for his *Joshua*. This was the boat he was racing around the world when he famously gave up victory, dropping out and setting sail for the South Seas. The design is still built under the name 'Joshua' in almost the original form.

Relevant to our purposes are the steering characteristics imparted by long keels. Boats of such a design hold a straight course very well, but if they should get away, the unbalanced rudder makes the steering force required to bring the boat back on to course quite substantial. They require servo-assisted windvane steering systems and reasonably sized autopilots. Manoeuvring these boats in harbour requires strong nerves and a cool head at the helm (or a couple of large fenders!).

Whether long-keel boats are safer and more seaworthy than boats with a shorter keel and a separate skeg-mounted rudder is a common topic of debate. The fact is that the relative stability in a sea at the same time makes rapid evasive action, for example to avoid breaking waves, considerably more difficult. The large lateral surface area of the long keel means that leeway is only slight in heavy weather, which increases the danger of capsize. The protected position of the rudder behind the keel and its solid attachment from top to bottom, however, could not be better from the point of view of safety.

Fin and skeg

The Sparkman & Stephens design office turned out a great many yachts in the 1960s and 1970s that are now considered to be classics. All old Swan yachts had a long fin keel and the rudder mounted separately on a robust skeg. The frame pattern was similar to that of the long-keel designs and V shaped frames were used here as well to ensure comfortable sailing, gentle motion and peace down below. These boats were likewise tremendously seaworthy, but

Left The hull lines of this Sparkman & Stephens guarantee comfortable sailing.

Below The seaworthiness of classic Colin Archer yachts is undisputed; *Hans Christian* moored in Chesapeake Bay in 1996.

Bottom A Concordia from Abeking & Rasmussen at Rockport Marina, Maine in 1996.

faster on account of their smaller wetted surface area and better behaved under engine – even in reverse.

A long fin keel is fairly easy to steer since, although the boat can be brought back on to course with less steering force, the keel still has sufficient surface area to keep the boat heading in a straight line. The steering forces required are less for this design than a long keel because the rudder blade has a balancing portion below the skeg. Fin and skeg boats are equally well suited to autopilots or windvane systems.

The fin and skeg configuration is clearly the preferred choice of the fleet of sailors passing through the Canary Islands bottleneck every year en route to warmer climes. All the classic cruising boats from Hallberg Rassy, Moody, Najad, Nicholson, Oyster, Amel and Westerly fall into this category. The very first grounding, collision with flotsam or storm is enough to convince every sailor of the significance of that strong skeg retaining and protecting the rudder.

Deep fin keel and balanced spade rudder

This configuration, which is widespread today, offers greater speeds and improved manoeuvrability in harbour. The hull frames are trapezoidal in the bow section and wide and flat towards the stern, a design that is good for length along the waterline (and hence speed) and that promotes surfing, but that reduces comfort on board. These boats do not carve through the waves, but rather bang hard against the water. They are noisy and uncomfortable to sail, but since the difference in comfort only becomes apparent on extended voyages the average sailor is unlikely to notice.

As far as the small contact area between keel and hull and the completely unprotected rudder are concerned, it seems astonishing that some skippers are prepared to set out on extended blue water voyages without even an emergency rudder on board.

Fin-keel boats are easily steered by windvane systems in as much as the boats are very responsive to the helm and steering impulses are therefore converted to course corrections promptly and quickly. The same applies to autopilots, although the more rapid yawing of some fin-keel boats can test the intelligence of the electronics to its limits.

Extreme yachts that are designed to plane are too much of a handful for windvane systems (see The ultimate limits of windvane steering, p 78): only the highest specification autopilot motors and hydraulic pumps have the power and speed necessary to keep them on course.

Centreboard or internal ballast

Boats of this design, in which the ballast is higher up, derive their basic stability from their width. They are consequently wider than other designs and more sensitive to trim. Increasing heel is almost always accompanied by increasing weather helm, which creates more work for either self-steering option.

The hull is generally of trapezoidal cross-section at the bow, which suggests a less comfortable ride at sea. A number of boats on the French market feature a small trimming rudder in addition to the internal ballast and are easier to trim as a result.

Top The hull lines of a modern yacht with a balanced rudder: fast, but not particularly comfortable.

Above The keel and rudder of this Dehler 36 are very susceptible to damage during grounding.

Left Boats with internal ballast perform well off the wind; a second centre-board makes trimming easier. This French Via 43, *Octopus,* went round the world with a Windpilot Pacific.

Multihulls

Catamarans

Catamarans have a relatively long length along the waterline and no ballast at all, and consequently hold a straight line very well. The pressure on the rudder is relatively low as well, so they are easily steered.

They accelerate far faster than monohulls in the puffs, however, which causes dramatic fluctuations in the apparent wind angle. The same is true in the lulls: they slow down quickly and the wind swings aft. The principle is as follows: when a gust hits a monohull, it causes increased heel and minor acceleration and the apparent wind swings forward only a little. A multihull is unaffected by heel but accelerates quickly; the apparent wind angle swings forward markedly.

This explains why catamaran sailors have always relied almost exclusively on autopilots. However, a windvane system can be useful on extended voyages.

Servo-pendulum systems can produce perfect steering on catamarans. The great speed potential allows the pendulum rudder to generate substantial steering force. The windvane functions well as the steering impulse generator as long as the wind strength and angle remain constant. It is no good in gusty weather or if the wind strength is variable because the windvane system will snake all over the place. In these conditions, the windvane can be removed and a small autopilot (cockpit autopilot) used to furnish the steering impulses.

A servo-pendulum system can obviously only function if steering force transmission to the main rudder is smooth. The steering lines should not under any circumstances be led via the wheel adaptor to a wheel steering system as the wheel is normally some way from the stern on a catamaran. Transmission to the emergency tiller works only if the wheel-steering mechanism can

This 15 m/48 ft catamaran moored off Las Palmas sailed around the world with a Windpilot Pacific.

be disconnected; this of course assumes that the helmsperson can easily reach (and steer with) the emergency tiller whenever it is necessary.

A better approach involves parting the mechanical connection between the two rudders, leaving rudder no. 1 connected to the wheel for manual steering and for fine trimming the course when the windvane system has the helm, and connecting rudder no. 2 to the servo-pendulum gear via the emergency tiller and the steering lines. Hydraulic steering systems can also be adapted by this method.

Auxiliary rudder and double rudder systems are not suitable for installation on catamarans. The aft beam crosses high above the surface so mounting the gear sufficiently close to the water proves difficult. Even if mounting on the aft beam was possible, it would still leave the auxiliary rudder completely exposed to flotsam.

Trimarans

The single rudder blade on a trimaran is much more easily controlled than the pair on a catamaran. Servo-pendulum systems can be used as long as the boat has tiller or mechanical wheel steering. Auxiliary rudder gears are less suitable because the outboard rudder of most trimarans makes proper positioning of the auxiliary rudder blade difficult. This type of gear also lacks the power required to cope with trimaran speeds. Double rudder systems are totally unsuitable. The two rudders of the gear would have to ride directly behind the outboard main rudder, and the auxiliary rudder would then be too close to the main rudder.

Rig: sloop, cutter, yawl or ketch

Traditional long-keel yachts were often yawl- or ketch-rigged to improve the balance of the sail plan. Especially in heavy weather, the foresail alone struggled to keep the boat

Yawl-rigged boats are always easy on the eye; this beautiful, traditional yacht was moored in Newport, Rhode Island in 1996.

tracking on course: increasing speed and heel pushed the centre of lateral resistance forward dramatically, generating substantial weather helm that had to be balanced out with a mizzen.

Blue water sailing today is dominated by fin and skeg boats (separate keel and rudder) on which the rudder and skeg are quite far aft. Their centre of lateral resistance does not wander to the same extent in response to rising boat speed or greater heel; they hold a course well and have no need of a second mast.

Indeed, all the hull configurations used today are able to deliver good all-round sailing performance without a second mast.

A mizzen staysail may well be a trouble-free and effective sail, but second masts cost money and increase the weight aloft. Not only that, but they are seldom used anyway because on typical trade wind courses the mizzen contributes more weather helm than drive. Most mizzen booms and sails will impair the functioning of a windvane, which

Left A mizzen that extends over the transom causes problems for a windvane.

Below A mizzen that stops at the transom is much more convenient.

prefers undisrupted air flow, and interfere with its turning radius. Most arguments for a second mast rest on other, unconnected factors: a mizzen mast provides a good site for antennas and radar and, most important of all, two masts look better in photographs!

The cutter rig probably provides the best compromise between good steering and uncomplicated boat-handling. It can be trimmed to balance just about every kind of boat and the distribution of the sail area over several relatively small sails makes boat-handling fairly straightforward even for small crews. Cutter-rigged masts also have a considerable safety advantage: the two additional stays, the backstay and the cutter stay, significantly reduce the risk of dismasting, a real confidence-booster in extreme conditions.

Swim ladders, swim platforms and davits

The presence of a swim ladder in the centre of the transom admittedly makes installing a windvane gear slightly less straightforward, but the swim ladder is not necessarily as important on long-distance voyages as some people think. The idea that a swim ladder is an essential means of recovering a crew member lost overboard sounds good in theory, but MOBs are most likely to occur when the sea is rough, the boat is bouncing around, and under the transom is a very dangerous place to be. The crew member would be better recovered over the side in these circumstances. Folding swim ladders stored in plastic boxes and positioned on both sides of the boat amidships would be a practical solution.

A swim platform is the perfect landing place on a long voyage and makes boarding the dinghy much easier when lying at anchor. It should ideally be about 50 cm/20 in above the water. Often standard on modern French designs, this feature only really comes into its own on a long trip. After a few rounds of struggling up the swim ladder with provisions or fuel cans, a sailor could easily come to covet his or her neighbour's platform! The platform is also good for showering in fresh water after a swim as it keeps the salt out of the boat. With proper planning it is quite possible to install a windvane gear and a swim platform at the same time.

Davits can be fitted in around a windvane gear given the following. An inflatable will spend the bulk of a long-distance trip either lashed to the deck or packed away and stowed. It would be irresponsible on an ocean

Ideal combination of swim platform and windvane gear on a Roberts 53.

Davits and a Pacific Plus are perfectly compatible on this HR 41 in Papeete.

French Ovni 43, moored in Las Palmas, ready for a long passage.

crossing to leave a tender exposed on davits to bad weather and big seas, and with the dinghy out of the way the windvane gear has all the space it needs. Modern windvane systems can be removed very quickly, so it is perfectly straightforward to swap between the tender and the gear as required. The pendulum rudder is the only part of the Windpilot Pacific Plus that could foul the tender, and this can be removed by undoing just one bolt. The auxiliary rudder does not interfere with the tender at all.

Following the suggestions above, it should be possible to combine swim platform, davits, offset-mounted swim ladder and windvane gear and still enjoy the full benefits of each. They all play very useful roles at various points of a blue water voyage and it would be a shame to have to manage without. The Pacific Plus

could even be partially integrated into the swim platform, given a little forethought, which amongst other things would help protect the auxiliary rudder when reversing. Even the pendulum unit could be protected: it is angled down and back by 10° in use, and therefore up and forward by the same amount in its raised position, so if the platform extended back to the shaft it would project beyond the raised pendulum rudder.

Consideration should also be given to the positioning of the various antennas. An equipment carrier with integrated davits such as that favoured by French Garcia yard is an ideal solution, putting the GPS, Inmarsat, radar and VHF antennas, solar panels and wind generator about 2 m/6½ ft above the deck. This position keeps them clear of the crew and ensures good reception, short cable paths to the receivers and, perhaps most importantly, protects the sensitive antennas from clumsy crew. Pushpit-mounted GPS antennas are forever being sat on or mistaken for convenient hand-holds.

A practical and visually unobjectionable solution can always be found provided the requirements of the various items to be fitted are properly assessed in the planning stage. Every subsequent addition or modification (eg davits, wind generator mast, etc) means extra weight and more unattractive clutter.

Mounting a windvane gear

Mounting a windvane gear on wooden, aluminium or steel boats poses no problems at all since all three materials have sufficient local strength. There is no real need to reinforce the inside of the transom, and those owners who do choose to do so mainly for the good of their nerves.

The inside of a composite hull transom, on the other hand, normally has no structural stiffening members and, depending on the particular boat and the system to be installed (weight, load distribution of mounting bracket), may well need reinforcing. The inside of a GRP hull with a sandwich laminate transom should always be reinforced around the mounting points with wood or similar before installing a windvane gear.

Important: Seal all the through hull fittings with silicone or sikaflex on the outside only. If you seal on the inside as well, it will be impossible to check for leakage in the outer sealing and any water entering will penetrate into the laminate undetected.

The fastening components of a windvane gear should always be through-bolted on a steel or aluminium hull. The alternative, welding reinforcing patches on to the outside of the transom so that the bolts can be accommodated in blind holes, will indeed prevent water leaking into the hull, but is very difficult to repair after a collision. It also causes substantial corrosion in steel hulls. Both steel and aluminium possess sufficient local material strength to support installation of a windvane gear without any extra stiffening measures.

Vessel size

Boats of 18 m/60 ft at present represent the upper limit of what can reliably be steered by a windvane steering system. Bigger boats rely almost exclusively on electronic systems; the heavy equipment and availability of auxiliary generators justifies the use of the most powerful autopilots.

Windpilot Pacific Light on a Crabber 24.

The corresponding lower limit seems to fall close to 5 m/18 ft, a length of boat not unheard of for extended voyages. A gear appropriate in other respects for a boat any shorter than this would, at around 20 kg/44 lb, be too heavy.

Man overboard function

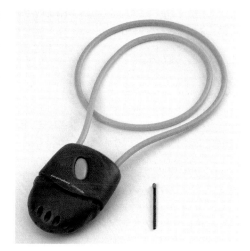

In England alone, 50 fishermen drowned after falling overboard in 1996 – which means, on average, almost one every week. The nightmare of parting company with the boat unintentionally haunts every sailor, and indeed every person who takes to the sea. It is a nightmare that often becomes reality, sometimes spectacularly as in the 1996 Vendée Globe, but more often completely unnoticed by the public (although no less painful for the bereaved). Only seldom does some guardian angel appear to pluck the unfortunates from the water.

Distress detection and rescue efforts span the globe to try and ensure that emergency assistance reaches those who need it before cold and exposure take their toll. There can be no feeling as lonely or absolutely terrifying as floundering in the wake of your boat as it sails off towards the horizon. The international maritime safety industry has for years been racing to develop a way of stopping a boat under autopilot steering.

The Emergency Guard system for autopilots appeared in Germany in 1996. Each crew member wears a small command set with a button and a sensor. If the button is pressed or the sensor is submerged, the command set sends a signal to the autopilot telling it to turn into the wind. The

The three modules of the Emergency Guard system.

autopilot has a dedicated clinometer which ensures that it turns into wind and never away from it. The foresail backs in this position and as soon as the clinometer registers heel to the other side, the autopilot puts the rudder hard over again, leaving the boat stationary apart from drift. This means in practice that the boat turns into the wind within five seconds of the system triggering and, depending on the speed and characteristics of the boat, the rudder is hard over and the boat speed indicator at zero within another 30 seconds.

The system can also be wired up to perform four additional tasks, namely:

1 Actuating an engine cut-off switch.
2 Triggering an audible alarm or the MOB function on the navigation instruments.
3 Activating an automatic rescue module (explosive-launched life-buoy and line).
4 Activating an EPIRB transmitter.

Emergency Guard comprises three components:

1 A command set worn around the neck on a loop. The loop also serves as the antenna. The coded signal prevents accidental operation by a foreign command set and has a range of about 600 m.
2 A controller that receives and passes on the signal. It can also be operated manually as well as by the signal.
3 A sensor unit, mounted below deck, which controls manoeuvring. The clinometer is highly sensitive, so care must be taken during installation to ensure the unit is absolutely level.

The system is also suitable for multihulls since the clinometer is sensitive enough to detect even the relatively slight heel they experience in response to wind pressure and also to eliminate the motion of the boat. Self-tacking foresails must be fixed in place for otherwise the foresail will not back.

A new feature of the Emergency Guard system, developed in collaboration with Windpilot, enables it to be used with the Pacific servo-pendulum gear. The signal from the command set is passed to a solenoid switch which uncouples the gear from the main rudder, leaving the boat to round up into the wind and stop.

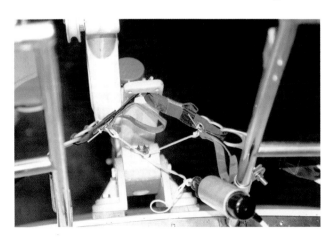

Emergency Guard solenoid switch on the Windpilot Pacific.

Summary

Every windvane steering system has precisely defined limits imposed by the level of technology it enjoys. Some systems, depending on their power leverage and damping properties and the characteristics of the boat, will hold out for longer than others, but sooner or later all will eventually lose control. Conservative reefing helps to put this moment off by reducing the magnitude of the course corrections required. A system with well-matched steering force and damping and a good reserve of power will always give better results than one that requires continuous manual tweaking to keep up with changing sea and weather conditions. Although the rudder pressure required to keep a boat on course is normally quite low, every sailor knows how rapidly things change in heavy weather or tradewinds sailing.

The perfect windvane gear possesses the sensitivity to steer in light airs and the power to cope with serious weather. Auxiliary rudders, with little or no servo-assistance, run out of answers relatively quickly. The enormous power reserves of servo-pendulum and double rudder gears facilitate effective steering over a far greater range of conditions. Choose the wrong system and you either steer by hand or return to port!

The best system from the crew's point of view would be one that works as a closed system, providing optimum steering without demanding endless manual adjustment. The greater the scope and need for manual adjustment to optimise steering, the more chances there are of error (human or mechanical). Ideally the crew should be able to concentrate exclusively on sail trim and the boat, and leave steering to the windvane gear.

With the steering handled by the windvane gear, there will be plenty of time to concentrate on sail trim on this Dutch 47 ft Judel Frolic.

• 7 •

Combination systems

Combining autopilot and windvane steering systems

Today, autopilots are often standard equipment on a boat. They are a good option for everyday use in weekend and holiday sailing, but the case in favour of a windvane steering system grows with the length of the planned voyage, especially when sailing with a small crew, and is virtually irresistible for ocean crossings. There can be no doubt, in the end, that the best self-steering solution for blue water sailing is to carry both an autopilot and a windvane gear.

There is one remarkably ingenious method of combining the advantages of the two systems which, despite having been described in detail at various times in just about all the major sailing publications, has still failed to get through to the majority of sailors. If a small push rod autopilot (eg Auto Helm 800) is connected to the counterweight of a servo-pendulum gear, it can be used to supply the steering impulse in place of the windvane. Amplification and transmission of the steering force take place as before. The autopilot can now steer the boat on a compass course with extremely low power consumption because the only force it has to supply is that normally sup-

plied by the windvane (ie that needed to rotate the pendulum rudder). Multiplying the steering force of the small Auto Helm 800 autopilot by the servo force of the pendulum rudder produces enough steering force at the main rudder to steer a boat of 25 tonnes. This combination is particularly useful in long following seas and a very light following breeze when the wind strength is insufficient to produce a proper signal from

A combination of autopilot and windvane steering system with remote control is ideal when cruising shorthanded.

A combination of Autohelm and Windpilot Pacific Plus on a Nicholson 48.

the vane but there is enough boat-speed to drive the servo-pendulum arrangement.

The autopilot/windvane gear synthesis manages in a practical sense to overcome the physical constants between input/output and electrical power/steering force outlined in Chapter 3.

An autopilot can be coupled, as described, to almost any windvane steering system:

Auxiliary rudder gear

The autopilot is coupled to the small emergency tiller, but there is no servo effect since in this system the windvane, and hence the autopilot, turns the auxiliary rudder directly. This arrangement is only called for if a

push rod autopilot cannot be connected to the main rudder tiller (eg wheel steering). An autopilot connected to the emergency tiller will often set up vibrations when motoring because the auxiliary rudder is in the turbulent wash from the propeller.

Servo-pendulum gear

The combination produces best results and is most easily realised with this kind of gear. The small retaining pin for the push rod system can be mounted anywhere on the windvane or counterweight. The maximum range of movement of the windvane or counterweight at this point must be greater than the lock-to-lock distance of the autopilot (Auto Helm, Navico: 25 cm/10 in), otherwise the windvane can sustain damage when the autopilot wants the rudder hard over.

Double rudder gear

The mechanical advantage of combining the systems is even greater here. The rudder of the boat to be steered, usually a relatively large boat if it has a double rudder gear, is used for fine-trimming the course so there is less pressure on the gear, allowing it to operate more precisely.

The small Auto Helm 800 system would in principle be able to manage all these arrangements, but the convenience of a handheld remote control contributes to the appeal of the Auto Helm 1000, the smallest push rod system with this option, and Navico's TP 100.

Years of experience have shown again and again that many blue water sailors, especially those with fewer miles under the keel, initially plan on installing just an autopilot. They choose a very powerful and robust system for safety and reliability. After a few days at sea, possibly before they are too far away from well-supplied ports, they then have a radical rethink. Sometimes a few night watches out on the ocean are enough to leave a crew yearning for a more straightforward solution, for example the comfortable and silent steering of a windvane gear.

The eventual conclusion that many yacht owners come to is that the powerful autopilot was an unnecessary investment; in the end, the wind is the better helm. They fit a small cockpit autopilot to the gear ready for the doldrums and are then equipped for anything. A combined windvane gear/cockpit autopilot system can often be put together for less money than an inboard autopilot, and will without a doubt rack up many many more hours at the helm.

Power generator/ autopilot hybrid

British company Windhunter has pioneered the idea of eliminating power consumption problems by combining a generator with a hydraulic pump set and ram. The system operates with a signal from a wind transducer or optional fluxgate compass. The hydraulic pump is installed at the back of an Aquair water generator. The oil circulated by the pump accumulates in the main module, from where it is diverted to the ram in accordance with the signal from the windvane to effect either port or starboard rudder movements. An Auto Helm fluxgate compass can be interfaced to allow compass-controlled steering. Although this synthesis might seem cleverly to circumvent typical autopilot problems, there are several points which require more detailed examination.

- All water generators cause drag. Driving the generator and hydraulic pump will magnify this drag. If a spinning propeller of around 25 mm/1 in diameter has to generate several amps/h, its drag can easily reach 30 to 45 kg/ 66 to 100 lb. The laws of physics dictate that energy generated by the movement of the boat through the water is paid for in boat speed. The boat will travel slower and the voyage will take longer; it is little wonder that so many sailing boats use a folding propeller.

- The problems familiar from conventional water generators will persist. The length of the rope on

Windhunter hybrid system components: generator with hydraulic oil pump, and wind transducer and oil pipes.

which the propeller trails, the speed of the boat and the height and length of the seas all affect generator performance. The pitch of the propeller must be matched to the speed of the boat, and it may sometimes be necessary to weight down the propeller shaft to prevent it from jumping out of the water. Sea conditions change continuously and acceleration and deceleration put strain on this kind of drive. Typical shock absorbers consisting of a number of ordinary ropes set up in the pushpit are not sufficient to absorb every shock. Shaft-mounted generators, which eliminate most of these problems, are common on larger yachts where the constant whine of the spinning propeller is accepted as the unavoidable consequence of the need to generate electricity. Any spinning propeller, whether towed or rigidly mounted on the transom, inevitably reduces both comfort and speed.

• The size and position of the windvane transducer which obtains the signal for the hydraulic valve have to be carefully considered to ensure proper functioning. The windvane transducer has a very small operating angle (only 0.5 mm of movement to either side from its vertical position). Disturbances in the airflow over the transducer, such as might be caused by the mainsail or by a spray hood or other fixture, can as a result, seriously impair the functioning of the system in windvane mode. It is very difficult to eliminate false steering signals caused by pitching, rolling and lateral motion of the boat and to provide proper damping. A certain adjustable deadband always has to

be set to avoid oversteering/excessive correction.

• The operating pressure of an inboard autopilot is such that only rigid, robustly mounted pipes or armoured flexible lines will do. Inboard autopilots also require special hydraulic oil and use metal ermeto couplings throughout. The Windhunter hybrid, on the other hand, uses normal engine oil (which needs regular changing) and manages with basic plastic tubes which can be bent and deformed after immersion in hot water. The tubes are joined together with simple plastic clamps and T pieces. This obviously suggests that the oil pressure generated by the propeller and hydraulic pump falls well short of the operating pressure applied to the rudder quadrant by an autopilot.

The pressure supplied by the pump in any hydraulic system must always be sufficient to maintain prolonged, powerful steering actions. Windhunter's representative has confirmed that a lack of power or falling pressure in this situation impairs steering performance. A conventional electrically driven inboard hydraulic pump allows higher and continuous pressure supply and hence faster and more powerful actions at the ram itself.

• Installation of the unit requires careful planning, particularly since the Windhunter ram, on account of its considerably lower operating pressure, cannot be integrated into a boat's existing hydraulic system. The Windhunter always requires a dedicated additional ram, which means at least two rams on the rudder quadrant for boats with hydraulic main steering.

Mechanical wheel steering Unless the system includes a solenoid or mechanical clutch to isolate the wheel steering transmission, the Windhunter's ram will have to move the whole existing steering arrangement from the wrong end every time it makes a course correction. This obviously impairs steering sensitivity. If a solenoid clutch is installed, it must be within easy reach of the crew in the cockpit in case it suddenly becomes necessary to resume manual steering.

Hydraulic wheel steering A bypass valve on the ram for the main rudder does not reduce the inertia of the ram itself, which will continue to hinder the Windhunter ram. The only way to overcome this problem effectively is to disconnect the main ram, a step which has potentially worrying safety implications. Any apparent gains made by interfering with a boat's existing steering arrangements have to be measured against one simple criterion, namely, how quickly can manual steering be restored. Immediate evasive steering action is virtually impossible with the main ram bypassed; fiddling around below deck to reconnect the ram or on the transom to operate the windvane directly costs precious seconds. The Windhunter system and the boat's own steering cannot both be operational at the same time without causing extensive damage.

• Installing the Windhunter is a far more involved process than installing an autopilot. The manufacturer's pitch of 'no holes in the hull' only holds if all the hoses and electric cables are led down through the companionway, which may be rather impractical, not to mention inconvenient. If the companionway does prove unsuitable, the additional holes necessary in the deck and cockpit area will need very careful sealing. The electrical power supply has to be fitted, the charging apparatus has to be integrated with the battery charge regulator, the control pad has to be mounted and wired up and the solenoid valves or mechanical connectors for the existing main steering ram and the self-steering ram have to be fitted (see Drive unit section in the Autopilots chapter). The ram itself needs a strong mounting on the inside of the hull (again see Drive unit section). Fitting the windvane transducer on the pushpit will be straightfoward by comparison since it weighs only 7 kg/ 16 lb. The whole system with generator, pump, ram, fillings, control system, oil, wind transducer and control pad, on the other hand, adds up to 50 kg/110 lb.

The Windhunter comes with a 55 page manual explaining in detail the set up procedure and the importance of calibrating the system for the idiosyncrasies of each particular boat. The five page Troubleshooting chapter includes advice on how to prevent oil leaks, on and below deck and into the sea, from damaging the teak and the environment. Plastic pipes and junctions, which if accidentally disturbed, leak oil and allow air into the hydraulic circuit, are not always ideal on the deck of a sailing boat.

DIY installation of the Windhunter is not straightforward and several steps involve working within the boat's electrical and mechanical/hydraulic systems.

The seven key parameters for comparing this type of autopilot hybrid with a conventional inboard autopilot are:

1 The ability of the hydraulic pump to supply effective and continuous pressure and the period over which this pressure can be maintained.
2 The drag of the generator.
3 The quality of the steering signals given by the transducers.
4 The availability of auto-adaptive components.
5 The technical aptitude of the owner and crew in fitting the system or the availability of qualified service mechanics.
6 The ease with which manual steering can be restored during an emergency.
7 The total price of the hybrid as compared with separate inboard autopilot and traditional generator.

Only time will show whether this generator/autopilot hybrid system will be able to match the currently preferred approach of running an intelligent inboard autopilot and generating electrical power separately (from the wind, water, sun, engine or generator). The Windhunter system is similar in terms of components to a conventional generator and inboard autopilot with the exceptions that its windvane transducer influences the hydraulic flow directly and the hydraulic pump is driven by water instead of electricity. The only feature the hybrid shares with windvane steering systems is the size of the windvane. The Windhunter windvane, however, is a simple transducer like those used by autopilots, and has none of the range of adjustment which makes vane gears so sensitive to the wind.

Windhunter hybrid components: **a)** The windvane bracket ony moves 0.5 mm. **b)** Generator with hydraulic oil pump. **c)** The six holes drilled in the deck have to be carefully sealed. **d)** The hydraulic ram needs a strong mounting.

· 8 ·

At a glance

System comparison: autopilots versus windvane steering systems

Autopilot: pros

- Invisible
- Compact
- Simple to operate
- Autopilot module can be integrated with navigation instruments
- Better price (cockpit autopilots)
- No interference with motoring
- Always ready to operate

Autopilot: cons

- Compass-derived steering impulse
- Consumes electricity
- Wind sensor less than ideal
- Delayed steering response
- Operating noise
- Technical reliability
- Limited life of transmission components
- Steering deteriorates as wind and sea conditions build
- Increased load on the rudder bearings (the helmsperson's arm gives a little to absorb shocks from the tiller; the push rod, in contrast, remains rigid, so the shocks are absorbed by the bearings)

Windvane steering system: pros

- Wind-derived steering impulse
- Uses no electricity
- Steering improves as wind and sea conditions build
- Immediate steering response
- Silent operation
- Mechanical reliability
- Solid construction
- Auxiliary rudder = emergency rudder
- Long service life
- Lower load on the rudder bearings (servo-pendulum gear) because the connection is not rigid

Windvane steering system: cons

- No use in a calm
- Operator error possible
- Some systems interfere with manoeuvring under engine
- Swim ladder may have to be moved (servo-pendulum system)
- Indiscreet
- Sometimes complicated to install

The differences between autopilot and windvane steering systems

	Autopilot	Windvane steering system	Synthesis
Data network	possible	not possible	possible
Steering impulse	compass	wind	compass/wind
Steering force	constant steering force/steering speed	progressive increase in steering force	both
Steering quality	deteriorates as wind/sea build	progressive as wind/sea build	both
Steering hours	breaks to reduce power consumption	steers continuously	both
Yawing angle	manually adjustable	depends on system	both
Ease of operation	push button	requires careful setting	

The ultimate limits of self-steering

No self-steering system can keep a boat under control all the time in all conditions. The operating ranges of the various systems we have discussed can all be expanded by careful trimming and prompt reefing – that is to say, by reducing heel and, in consequence, the rudder movement required to keep the boat on course. These measures almost always yield better boat speed combined with better steering accuracy from the self-steering system.

The performance of a windvane steering system actually improves as wind and sea conditions build.

Self-steering under sail means relaxing sailing with no work at the helm on this 40 ft Dutch Carena.

Every self-steering system has its own performance profile; it always delivers the same steering force in the same conditions. Differences in performance arise as a result of the characteristics of the vessel to be steered and, in particular, as a result of the willingness of the crew to trim the sails properly (of course they generally have ample time and opportunity to do so).

The importance of sail trim

The effects of poor sail trim are equally detrimental to both types of self-steering system. Poor trim for an autopilot means more pressure on the main rudder, more taxing operating conditions (because more forceful rudder movements are needed) and, as a result, increased power consumption. The system's reserves of power and travel decline and yawing movements increase; the autopilot loses control sooner.

Poor trim similarly reduces the power and travel reserves of a windvane system. Poor sail trim means weather helm – sailing with the handbrake on.

· 9 ·

The present situation

We have now discussed all the various systems invented to date. After 30 years of development, the market offers the following options:

Autopilot

- Cockpit autopilot
- Inboard autopilot

Windvane steering system

- Auxiliary rudder gear
- Servo-pendulum gear
- Double rudder gear

Combined cockpit autopilot/windvane steering system

The key criteria governing the choice of system are determined by the size of boat to be steered. Boats are classified to this end according to:

Size

- Up to 9 m/30 ft
- Up to 12 m/40 ft
- Up to 18 m/60 ft
- Over 18 m/60 ft

Design

- Long keel
- Long fin keel and skeg
- Deep fin keel and balanced spade rudder
- Centreboard or internal ballast
- ULDB
- Multihull

Speed potential

- Planing boat, yes/no ?

Steering

- Tiller
- Wheel, mechanical
- Wheel, hydraulic

Cockpit positioning

- Aft
- Centre

Use

- Holidays and weekends
- Coastal sailing
- Blue water sailing
- Racing

Trends

Somewhere between 80 and 90 per cent of all sea-going sailing yachts now have an autopilot. Raytheon, which manufactures the Autohelm range, has the biggest share of the combined world market. The company is responsible for a considerable proportion of the development work done on yacht autopilots and is the market leader in cockpit autopilots. It shares the inboard autopilots sector with the Norwegian producer Robertson, which concentrates on fitting out merchant ships and is the market leader for very large yachts, and the British company Brookes & Gatehouse.

It took 20 years for simple push rod autopilots to evolve into the computer controlled, network-integrated navigation modules produced today, a striking measure of how much things have changed on board in less than a generation. This is a powerful reminder, as well, of how even our most advanced technology still bows down before the principles of physics. Somehow, as many sailors have come to understand, these principles seem to have sharper claws out at sea.

Engineering defects in an autopilot almost always mean manual steering, an exhausting prospect when you are far from land. A quick look at the list in the Las Palmas ARC office of competitors requesting autopilot servicing before the start of the race every November confirms how often systems break down. The manufacturers' engineers, who always fly out from England for the event, labour tirelessly and never find themselves short of work. Many of the boats carry a back-up system as well, just in case.

Compared to the rapid pace of development in autopilots, the progress of windvane steering has been snail-like. Most of the systems on the market today have remained virtually unchanged from the day they were introduced. One possible explanation for this is the fact that most of the manufacturers are too small to be able to finance new projects, particularly since research and development now involves such high costs. On the other hand, though there is almost certainly an element of inertia, there is also a reluctance to change a product that still sells. Finally, some manufacturers simply do not engage in design innovation, preferring instead to find their inspiration in the products of those who do push back the boundaries in this sector of the market. Given that the customer is generally quite critical and demanding, such copycat manufacturers tend, as history has shown, to find the market rather tough.

If the belief persists amongst some in the sailing world that an Aries is simply the ideal servo-pendulum gear, this may well be because most sailors simply have no knowledge of the different systems available and therefore have no way of making proper product comparisons. All the major servo-pendulum gear manufacturers who use a bevel gear linkage now in fact employ identical kinematic transmission ratios. Their products do, though, differ considerably in terms of execution, method of manufacture and styling.

The rapid spread of the electric competition put some mechanical windvane gear manufacturers into reflective mood, even if the glossy brochures promising autopilot steering for large and heavy boats for less than 1 amp at least irritated a good number of sailors. The sometimes heated debate over the advantages and disadvantages of the two systems continued for many years. Now sailors have a very much clearer picture of the pros and cons of all the options and are well aware of the heightened importance of good self-steering on longer voyages.

The definition of what constitutes a good windvane steering system has changed dramatically over the last 25 years. At first, any system that managed to keep a boat on something approximating the desired course was considered a success, and rustic appearance, excessive weight, awkward handling and frequent servicing were not handicaps. Today, windvane steering system manufacturers compete in a market where the customer is quite able to distinguish between products, and will weigh everything against the simplicity of an autopilot: control at the touch of a button!

One interesting observation that deserves mentioning is that almost everybody who considers purchasing (or does purchase) a windvane gear already has an autopilot. Once installed, however, the windvane shoulders up to 80 per cent of the burden and the autopilot hardly comes on at all when the sails are up. Jimmy Cornell has confirmed these findings based on the debriefings we mentioned earlier. The tendency of yachts to carry both types of system has become ever more pronounced over the ten ARC races that have now been held. Windvane steering systems are still as important as ever for reliable steering on long-distance short-handed trips.

Practical tips

Using the criteria presented in this book you should be in a position to choose a windvane steering system for yourself, and the same goes for a cockpit autopilot. If you are looking at an inboard autopilot, on the other hand, you will need the help of an expert for the calculations with regard to rudder area, pressure or load that are normally part of the ordering process with the major manufacturers. These help to determine the drive unit required.

It will quickly become apparent on reading the market summary that follows that the whole self-steering market has undergone considerable concentration in recent years. Few companies are now capable of the international marketing, with its multilingual brochures and constant presence at the international boat shows, that catches the eye and wins the confidence of the potential customer. Autohelm, B & G, Robertson, Hydrovane, Monitor and Windpilot are the manufacturers who visit all the European shows and offer good and prompt customer service. They are also the companies whose systems are sufficiently well known and regarded to guarantee the continuity of the business.

The number of companies that have shut down over the years illustrates how discerning the customer is in this market. A good product alone is not enough. Reliable advice and good personal service are the basis of this delicate business in which honesty and realistic promises are more important than big words that disappear on the breeze as soon as you leave harbour. Written warranties may work well as an advertising technique, but they are very little use when something actually does go wrong if the sailor suddenly finds, for example, that he or she must first prove that negligence on board was not the cause. What counts in such a situation is quick and unbureaucratic assistance so that the voyage can continue; a broken windvane gear can very easily rubbish an itinerary. A delay while the manufacturer requests document after document to try and save some money does the customer no good at all. Good word-of-mouth publicity amongst sailors is what every manufacturer strives for, and building up the necessary base of satisfied customers takes years of

good service and support. Once there, however, the systems all but sell themselves!

The point to remember in this respect is that even one unsatisfied customer can, in the course of a trip, express his or her dissatisfaction often enough to trigger a flood of adverse publicity which even the glossiest full-page adverts could not mop up. The only way to ensure continued good business is to cultivate a 'fan club' in the sailing community: the sea does not tolerate poor advice, and the results are impossible to overlook, for example, when manual steering becomes essential because the automatic system has failed.

The start of the 1996 ARC from Las Palmas.

It is curious that sailors seem to have a split personality when it comes to warranties. Faults in an autopilot are accepted more or less silently and it is often impossible to assess the accuracy of manufacturers' promises regarding modifications, improved quality and hence better durability until after the warranty has expired. The demands on a windvane steering system are normally somewhat greater: owners often expect the gear to be virtually perfect for the whole of its life. The tiny number of used systems available on the market (excepting those smaller systems shed as an owner moves on to a bigger boat) suggests how satisfied customers are even over the longer term.

The major companies in the market have earned their success through endurance, regular presence at the shows and good references from demanding customers. The table below, showing the prevalence of the different windvane steering systems in the ARC fleet over the last two races, gives a fairly accurate idea of which systems are currently popular.

Windvane steering systems in the ARC

System	1994	1995
Aries	5	7
Atoms	–	2
Hydrovane	7	7
Monitor	5	5
Mustafa	1	–
Navik	1	2
Sailomat	–	3
Windpilot	13	18

Distribution

The gap between autopilots and windvane steering systems in this respect could hardly be larger. Because of the large market volume, autopilots are offered via global distribution networks in which direct contact between manufacturer and customer is virtually non-existent. Only large manufacturers have the resources to set up and maintain a worldwide service network, an important consideration for sailors on a long trip. The major manufacturers visit all the big boat shows.

Windvane steering systems are almost always sold directly. Personal contact between manufacturers and sailors is normal and the customer's confidence is often based on it. Because we live in the age of Inmarsat, fax, e-mail, UPS, DHL and airfreight, there is no corner of the world with which direct communication and supply are impossible. Manufacturer beware – if your products fall short of the mark, there is nowhere left to hide!

The author (left) and Hans Bernwall of Monitor at the 1996 London Boat Show.

• 10 •
Technical information

Technical specifications of selected cockpit autopilots

Make	Auto Helm							Navico			
Type	AH800	ST1000	ST2000	ST4000T	ST4000GP	ST 3000	ST4000W	TP100	TP300	WP100	WP300CX
Voltage	12 V	12 V	12 V	12 V	12 V	12 V	12 V	12 V	12 V	12 V	12V
Average power cons. standby 25 % duty	0.06 A / 0.5 A	0.06 A / 0.5 A	0.06 A / 0.5 A	0.06 A / 0.7 A	0.06 A / 0.7 A	0.06 A / 0.7 A	0.06 A / 0.75 A	0.06 A / 0.5 A	0.06 A / 0.5 A	0.06 A	0.06A
Helm speed lock to lock: no load / 20 kg/44 lb load / 40 kg/88 lb load	6.7 sec / 9.6 sec / –	6.7 sec / 9.6 sec / –	4.1 sec / – / 6.4 sec	3.9 sec / – / 5.8 sec	4.3 sec / – / 5.5 sec	– / – / –	– / – / –	6.5 sec / 9.0 sec / –	4.2 sec / 6.0 sec / –		
Drive thrust	15 kg/ 33 lb	57 kg/ 125 lb	77 kg/ 169 lb	84 kg/ 185 lb	93 kg/ 205 lb	–	–	65 kg/ 143 lb	85 kg/ 187 lb		
Push rod travel	25 cm/ 10 in	25 cm/ 10 in	25 cm/ 10 in	25 cm/ 10 in	25 cm/ 10 in	–	–	25 cm/ 10 in	25 cm/ 10 in		
Wheel speed	–	–	–	–	–	3.3 rpm	5.5 rpm	–	–		
Max. wheel torque	–	–	–	–	–	70 Nm	75 Nm	–	–		
Max. revolutions	–	–	–	–	–	up to 3.5	up to 3.5	–	–		
Remote control operation	No	Yes	Yes	Yes	Yes	Yes	Yes	No	Yes	Yes	Yes
Suitable for boats up to	2 tonnes	2 tonnes	3.5 tonnes	5.5 tonnes	9 tonnes	5.5 tonnes	6.5 tonnes	2.8 tonnes	5.5 tonnes		
Off course alarm	Yes	Yes	Yes	Yes	Yes	Yes	Yes	No	Yes	No	Yes
Deadband contr.	Yes	Yes	Yes	Yes	Yes	Yes	Yes	Yes	Yes	Yes	Yes
Reversible	Yes	Yes	Yes	Yes	Yes	Yes	Yes	Yes	Yes	Yes	Yes
Gain adjustable	No	Yes	Yes	Yes	Yes	Yes	Yes	Yes	Yes	Yes	Yes
Auto tack	Yes	Yes	Yes	Yes	Yes	Yes	Yes	Yes	Yes	Yes	Yes
Compass callibr.	No	Yes	Yes	Yes	Yes	Yes	Yes	Yes	Yes	Yes	Yes

The 12 types of windvane steering system

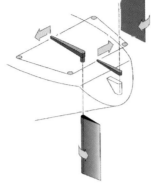

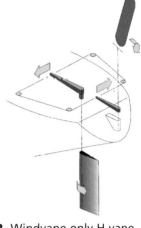

1 Windvane only V vane

2 Windvane only H vane

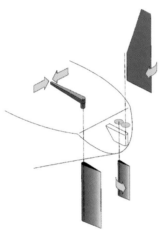

3 Auxiliary rudder V vane

4 Auxiliary rudder H vane

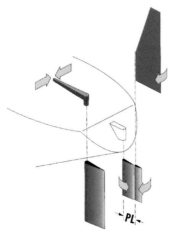

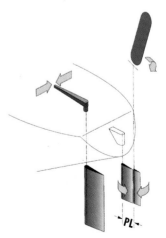

5 Trim tab on auxiliary rudder V vane

6 Trim tab on auxiliary rudder H vane

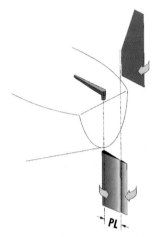

7 Trim tab on main rudder
  V vane

8 Trim tab on main rudder
  H vane

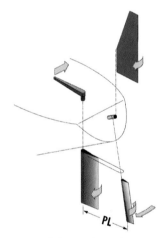

9 Pendulum trim tab V vane

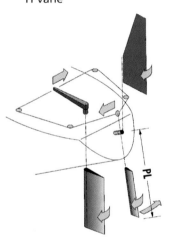

10 Servo-pendulum V vane

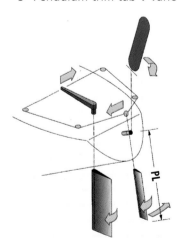

11 Servo-pendulum H vane

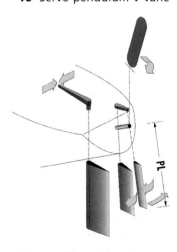

12 Double rudder H vane

Summary of the 12 types of system

No	Type	Brand	Country of origin	Vane type	Servo power	Power leverage	Bevel gear	Vessel size	Still in production
1	vane only	Windpilot Nordsee	Ger	V	no	0	no	< 6 m/20 ft	no
2	vane only	QME	GB	H	no	0	no	< 7 m/23 ft	no
3	auxiliary rudder	Windpilot Atlantik 2/3/4	Ger	V	no	0	no	< 10 m/33 ft	no
		Windpilot Caribic 2/3/4	Ger	V	no	0	no	< 10 m/33 ft	no
4	auxiliary rudder	Hydrovane	GB	H	no	0	no	< 15 m/49 ft	yes
		Levanter	GB	H	no	0	no	< 12 m/39 ft	no
5	trim tab/ auxiliary rudder	RVG	USA	V	yes	< 25 cm/10 in	no	< 12 m/39 ft	no
6	trim tab/ auxiliary rudder	Auto Helm	USA	H	yes	< 25 cm/10 in	no	< 12 m/39 ft	yes
		BWS Taurus	NL	H	yes	< 20 cm/8 in	no	< 15 m/49 ft	yes
		Mustafa	I	H	yes	< 25 cm/8 in	no	< 18 m/60 ft	yes
7	trim tab/ main rudder	Hasler trim tab	GB	V	yes	< 50 cm/20 in	no	< 12 m/39 ft	no
		Windpilot Pacific trim tab	Ger	V	yes	< 50 cm/20 in	no	< 12 m./39 ft	no
8	trim tab/ main rudder	Atlas	F	H	yes	< 50 cm/20 in	no	< 10 m/33 ft	no
		Auto-Steer	GB	H	yes	< 50 cm/20 in	no	< 12 m/39 ft	yes
		Viking Roer	S	H	yes	< 50 cm/20 in	no	< 12 m/39 ft	no
9	trim tab/ pendulum rudder	Saye's Rig	USA	V	yes	< 100 cm/39 in	no	< 18 m/60 ft	yes
		Quartermaster	GB	V	yes	< 100 cm/39 in	no	< 10m/33 ft	no
10	servo- pendulum rudder	Hasler	GB	V	yes	< 150 cm/59 in	no	< 12 m/39 ft	no
		Schwingpilot	Ger	V	yes	< 50 cm/20 in	no	< 12 m/39 ft	no
		Windpilot Pacific Mk I	Ger	V	yes	< 140 cm/55 in	yes	< 14 m/46 ft	no

		System	Country			Size		Max vessel size	
11	servo-pendulum rudder	Aries Standard	GB	H	yes	190 cm/75 in	yes	< 18 m/60 ft	yes
		Aries Lift-Up	GB	H	yes	190 cm/75 in	yes	< 18 m/60 ft	no
		Aries Circumnavigator	GB	H	yes	190 cm/75 in	yes	< 18 m/60 ft	no
		Atoms	F	H	yes	140 cm/55 in	no	< 12 m/39 ft	no
		Atlas	F	H	yes	140 cm/55 in	no	< 12 m/39 ft	no
		Auto-Steer	GB	H	yes	160 cm/ 63 in	yes	< 15 m/49 ft	yes
		Bogassol	E	H	yes	139 cm/51 in	no	< 12 m/39 ft	yes
		Bouvaan	NL	H	yes	120–150 cm/47–579 in	no	< 12 m/39 ft	yes
		Cap Horn	Can	H	yes	120–150 cm/47–59 in	no	< 14 m/46 ft	yes
		Fleming	NZ	H	yes	130–170 cm/51–67 in	yes	< 18 m/60 ft	yes
		Monitor	USA	H	yes	160 cm/ 63 in	yes	< 18 m/60 ft	yes
		Navik	F	H	yes	140 cm/55 in	no	< 10 m/33 ft	yes
		Super Navik	F	H	yes	170 cm/ 67 in	no	< 13 m/43 ft	yes
		Sailomat 601	S	H	yes	140–210 cm/55–83 in	no	< 18 m/60 ft	no
		Sirius	NL	H	yes	150 cm/59 in	yes	< 13 m/43 ft	no
		Windtrakker	GB	H	yes	170 cm/67 in	yes	< 15 m/49 ft	yes
		Windpilot Pacific Light	Ger	H	yes	140 cm/55 in	yes	< 9 m/30 ft	yes
		Windpilot Pacific	Ger	H	yes	160–220 cm/63–86 in	yes	< 18 m/60 ft	yes
12	double rudder	Stayer/Sailomat 3040	S	H	yes	130 cm/51 in	no	< 12 m/39 ft	no
		Windpilot Pacific Plus	Ger	H	yes	160–220 cm/63–86 in	yes	< 18 m/60 ft	yes

Definitions

Power leverage = PL (see illustrations) This provides an indication of the steering force obtainable from a system. The longer the lever is, the greater the steering force and, therefore, the better the steering performance will be.

Servo power is generated by harnessing the force of the water flowing past the hull (boat speed).

Vessel size (see manufacturer's specifications) The actual capabilities of a system with respect to maximum vessel size are subject to certain limitations (point 1).

Remember: What is the use of a system that can steer a boat in only 60–70 per cent of likely conditions and gives up off the wind whenever the wind is very light or very strong?

V vane yaw damping This is provided by limited rotational deflection of vane, maximum = angle of the deviation from course.

H vane yaw damping This is provided by a bevel gear linkage with 2:1 step-down ratio; automatic yaw damping, so oversteering is impossible. Systems without perfect damping require more manual trim corrections from the crew.

Technical data of selected windvane steering systems

	Operating principle			Windvane		Material			Bearings	Yaw damping by	Installed weight (kg/lb)	Bolts needed for installation
	AR	SP	DR	Type	Angle adjustable?	Windvane	System	Rudder				
Aries STD		+		H	yes	plywood	aluminium	GRP	sliding	bevel gear	35/77	8
Hydrovane	+			H	yes	aluminium/Dacron ®	aluminium	moulded plastic	ball and sliding	3 position linkage	approx 33/73	4–6
Monitor		+		H	no	plywood	stainless steel	stainless steel	ball and needle	bevel gear	approx 28/62	16
Navik		+		H	no	thermoplastic	stainless steel	GRP	sliding	–	19/42	8
Stayer/ Sailomat 3040			+	H	no	foam	aluminium	GRP/ aluminium	needle	axle angled aft	35/77	8
Sailomat 601		+		H	no	plywood	aluminium	aluminium	needle/ ball	axle angled aft	24/53	4
Schwingpilot		+		V	–	GRP	aluminium	aluminium	sliding	V-vane	28/62	8
WP Atlantik	+			V	–	stainless steel/Dacron ®	stainless	GRP/ stainless	sliding	V-vane	35/77	4
WP Pacific Light		+		H	yes	plywood	aluminium	wood	sliding	bevel gear	13/29	4
WP Pacific		+		H	yes	plywood	aluminium	wood	sliding	bevel gear	20/44	4
WP Pacific Plus			+	H	yes	plywood	aluminium	wood/GRP	sliding	bevel gear	40/88	8

KEY
AR = auxiliary rudder system
SP = servo-pendulum system
DR = double rudder system
WP = Windpilot

Technical data of selected windvane steering systems

	Remote control	Rudder blade not in use	Possible emergency rudder	Bolts to undo to remove system	Wheel adaptor adjustable by	Sizes available	Suitable for for vessels up to
Aries STD	+	no lift up	no	8	toothed wheel	1	18 m/60 ft
Hydrovane	option	fixed or removable	yes	4	–	1	approx 50 ft
Monitor	+	pivots aft	no	4	latch pin	1	18 m/60 ft
Navik	+	disconnect and pull up	no	4	–	1	approx 33 ft
Stayer/ Sailomat 3040	+	drops out downwards	yes	2	–	3	18 m/60 ft
Sailomat 601	+	lift up	no	1	fixed drum	1	18 m/60 ft
Schwingpilot	+	drops out downwards	no	4	–	1	approx 40 ft
WP Atlantik	–	fixed	yes	2	–	3	10 m/35 ft
WP Pacific Light	–	lift up	no	1	infinite	1	30 ft
WP Pacific	+	lift up	no	1	infinite	1	60 ft
WP Pacific Plus	+	lift up	yes	2	–	2	40ft 60 ft

KEY

AR = auxiliary rudder system
SP = servo-pendulum system
DR = double rudder system
WP = Windpilot

A to Z of manufacturers

Autopilots

Alpha

This American-based company is manufacturing robust basic autopilots which are renowned for their power efficiency. Interfaced to a PC they can process all onboard electronic information.

Autohelm

Founded in 1974 by British engineer Derek Fawcett, Autohelm has expanded continuously and has been the world-wide market leader from day one.

The characteristic six-button operating pad was introduced in 1984 and remains unchanged: Auto – autopilot on; +1/+10 – add 1°/10° to the heading; –1/–10 – subtract 1°/10° from the heading; and Standby.

Autohelm merged in 1990 with Raytheon Inc, an American multinational with 70 000 employees and interests in everything from refrigerators to autopilots to rockets, and launched its own data bus and data transfer protocol shortly afterwards.

Sea Talk (ST) denotes systems that are equipped to use this data bus. A simple single cable connection links all the system components together, allowing them to exchange wind, log, GPS and nav-centre data. Autohelm still leads the field in this area, and all its systems (apart from the AH 800) are ST compatible and can be linked to other modules. All systems have NMEA 0183 interfaces. Autohelm systems are produced at the company's site in England, which employs about 300 workers. The company currently has about 90 per cent of the market for cockpit autopilots, and about 50–60 per cent of the market for inboard autopilots for sailing yachts up to 18 m/60 ft. The most important inboard units for sailboat use are the ST 6000 and ST 7000. The ST 7000 has larger displays and an analogue rudder sensor; both are auto-adaptive pilots which can also be adjusted by the user.

Autohelm has a worldwide distribution network with service centres around the globe.

Benmar

This is an American manufacturer with only a limited presence in Europe. Benmar supplies autopilots for many 12 m/40 ft motor yachts in the USA.

Brookes & Gatehouse

The English company Brookes & Gatehouse (B & G) was founded only a year after the birth of the transistor and the onset of the electronics revolution. The company rose to prominence thanks to two legendary instrument ranges, Homer and Heron, which appeared on virtually all the bigger yachts of the day. Continuous development in the field of onboard electronics for the discerning sailor has helped the company retain a sizeable share of this market. B & G competes internationally with a full range of integrated instruments. The Network Pilot is the basic model. The Hydra links all the modules together, providing for extremely fast reaction via its own high speed data bus. The latest addition to the range, the Hy-Pro, is a refined hydraulic autopilot with integrated or separately available modules to gather data on a whole range of relevant parameters. B & G is probably the only manufacturer to offer a CD Rom manual. The Hydra and Hercules Pilot autopilot systems are available in a range of specifications and sizes and are predominantly found on larger boats.

B & G systems are used in all the big races (Whitbread, Fastnet, Sydney–Hobart, America's Cup, Admiral's Cup), where the emphasis is squarely on the company's excellent transducer and tactical processing systems for wind, log, depth and navigation data.

B & G has a worldwide distribution and service network.

Navico

The only challenger to Autohelm in some parts of the world, Navico has been producing its Tillerpilot 100 and 300 models for some years and has recently moved into wheelpilots. The WP 100 and WP 300 CX are well designed and offer a good selection of features. The company's original inboard pilot, the PL8000, has been superseded by the new Oceanpilot series, which has large displays and an integral rudder sensor. Oceanpilot units are auto-adaptive but have manually adjustable gain and a sail/power option. Navico also provides a full range of integrated instruments.

Navico has subsidiaries in France, Britain and the USA.

Cetrek

Another well-known name and one of the pioneers in the autopilot industry, this English manufacturer also fits out commercial vessels. Cetrek invented the auto-compensating compass and has pioneered the control algorithms known as 'fuzzy logic'. Presently owned by Teleflex, a specialist in all areas of maritime steering, Cetrek offers a complete range of data-linked instrument modules for the recreational sailor. The company's C-NET 780 model is auto-adaptive and features auto-learning, auto-phasing and a menu of 20 functions including a choice between 'planing' and 'displacement speed' settings.

Cetrek is based in the UK and has subsidiaries in the USA.

Coursemaster

This Australian manufacturer has a good reputation for rugged autopilots. All kinds of drive are available. The units rely more on manual adjustment.

Neco

This English company also has a background in commercial shipping.

Neco expanded into the yacht autopilot sector for a few years, but has now returned to its core business.

Robertson

Robertson was founded in 1946 and initially concentrated on the manufacture of autopilots for commercial fishing, a market it quickly came to dominate. Norwegian Simrad Robertson AS is now market leader in fitting out and automation for commercial and offshore shipping. Its products range from complete steering and navigation systems for supertankers to single autopilot systems for small commercial fishing boats.

The expansion into recreational sailing was a logical step since autopilot systems developed for the rigours of commercial operation were also highly suitable for sailing boats; looking at the high-tech bridge of a modern ocean-going trawler, the ancestry of our yacht autopilots is plain to see. Robertson's first yacht autopilot, the AP 22, was introduced in 1973. Self-adjusting autopilots were essential for commercial shipping and, once available, quickly became standard.

The capabilities of modern yacht autopilots may seem amazing, but they are really just hand-me-downs from commercial shipping, where the demands placed on (and indeed met by) continuously operating autopilots are of an entirely different magnitude.

Robertson autopilots are known for great robustness and are particularly common on larger vessels. They probably enjoy the lion's share of the worldwide market for maxis and big motor yachts. Most popular are the AP300X and AP300CX systems, which have adaptive programs, integral rudder sensors and oversize displays. Both use an arrangement whereby the fluxgate compass signal is converted into a frequency signal. This frequency signal is easier to process and consequently yields better steering commands. In 1997 a new product line, the AP20, was introduced.

Distribution is via the company's own worldwide network of subsidiaries and service centres.

Segatron

This small-volume high-quality German manufacturer has been in existence for some 28 years now. The company and its five employees build a small number of premium autopilots every year, predominantly for use on maxis, including Jongert yachts. Segatron systems naturally incorporate an NMEA interface to allow integration into an onboard data network.

Silva

This Swedish manufacturer recently introduced a data bus compatible inboard autopilot with several drive unit options. The A1500 autopilot can be data-linked with Nexus instruments and has an NMEA interface for GPS and wind transducer. Silva's drive units, previously marketed as Wagner Pilots, have a good reputation as strong, reliable, commercially used hardware.

VDO

VDO is a German company and a subsidiary of Mannesman AG. Originally built up as an instrument manufacturer for the automotive industry, it has been active in the marine sector for some time. VDO launched its VDO Logic line, another integrated instrument system, in 1993.

VDO systems are distributed through branches in Germany, Austria and Switzerland.

Vetus

A big name in the watersports industry, this Dutch manufacturer has for some years been marketing a range of British-built autopilots under the name Vetus Autopilot. These systems are also data bus compatible. The range includes a large selection of mechanical and hydraulic drive units.

Windhunter

This UK-based company has been marketing a generator/autopilot hybrid system since the mid-1990s. Windhunter and its representatives are very secretive about their product and its core 'fluid-logic' technology and have been unwilling to supply in-depth information: 'Your questions go far beyond what you need to know to write about Windhunter in your book'. Neither the American sales manager nor the manufacturer has been prepared to explain in particular how the unit's hydraulic management system actually works. One representative did however state that in light of the problems associated with generators driven by a towed propeller, the company had decided to offer a captive transom-mounted turbine. Several of the options mentioned in the price list are no longer available and it appears likely that eventually only the full autopilot/generator/windvane/data-linked compass transducer set will be available.

Windhunter: to avoid hoses and cables running along the companionway, about six holes will need to be drilled in the deck.

Windvane steering systems

Aries (system type 11)

Nick Franklin started building the Aries servo-pendulum system in Cowes, Isle of Wight, in 1968. Bronze was originally used for the unit, but was replaced by aluminium fairly early on. The Aries gears in production shortly before Franklin closed up the business in the late 1980s were still almost identical in appearance to the very first units. Characteristic of Aries systems is the toothed wheel course setting mechanism with increments of 6°. One story suggests that this component was never modified because a giant milling machine, so big that the roof of the workshop had to be raised to accommodate it, had initially been

Nick Franklin, designer of the Aries servo-pendulum system.

Aries Lift-Up.

installed to machine it, and a subsequent change in the toothed wheel design would have negated all the work.

The Aries gear was carried on a number of legendary voyages and came to epitomise for sailors the robustness and indestructibility of mechanical servo-pendulum systems – even though it had some glaring weaknesses in practice. The push rod connecting the windvane to the bevel gear, a solid casting, was overbuilt and the system suffered in lighter winds as a consequence. The push rod never experiences high loads as its only function is to transmit the force from the windvane which rotates the pendulum rudder. The 6° increments of the course setting mechanism are not always sufficiently fine going to weather: 6° can be the

difference between sailing too deep and backing the sails.

The Aries Standard pendulum rudder is complicated to connect and disconnect and, since it cannot normally be raised up out of the water, requires great care when reversing. These drawbacks meant that the systems were not particularly suitable for everyday use on shorter voyages and led later to the development of the Aries Lift-Up. Once the whole windvane support had been disassembled, the body of this modified gear could be released and then pivoted up and forwards. Although undoubtedly an improvement, the solution was still not ideal since the gear was completely unsecured on the mounting during the pivoting up procedure, a potentially dangerous situation in a sea.

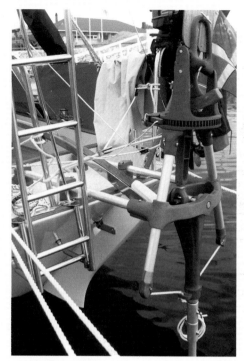

Aries Standard.

material costs and an increasingly difficult market, and because he had finally finished building his own boat and was ready, after 20 years of the stress of a full-time job, to head for more peaceful waters.

Spare parts for all Aries systems are available from Franklin's daughter Helen, directly from England.

The Aries Standard has recently been resurrected by Dane Peter Mathiessen in Nordborg. Mathiessen uses aluminium parts made in England and machines them in metric sizes. The one available system is specified for boats of up to 18 m/60 ft and can be obtained directly from the manufacturer.

Atlas

This windvane gear was built for many years in France and came in three versions:

- Trim tab on main rudder (system type 8)
- Trim tab on auxiliary rudder (system type 6)
- Servo-pendulum (system type 11)

None of the systems had bevel gear yaw damping and all consequently required very precise trimming of the boat. Production ceased at the end of the 1980s following the untimely death of the manufacturer.

Atoms

The Atoms servo-pendulum gear (system type 11) was produced in Nice, France, for many years and was very popular in its home waters. The distinctive features of this system were the aluminium windvane and the circular segment connecting the steering lines to the pendulum rudder which ensured uniform force

The Aries Circumnavigator, basically an Aries Standard with a better mounting and a removable pendulum rudder, was introduced in the mid-1980s. The wheel coupling uses a finely toothed wheel, allowing good adjustment and setting.

Despite its disadvantages, the Aries system has often been the subject of imitation by manufacturers happy to forgo the trials of innovation and shelter in the lee of the excellent reputation of the original.

A considerable part of the success of Aries must be put down to the highly personable nature of Nick Franklin himself. Set in the beautiful Isle of Wight countryside, he and his company were always a competent business partner for sailors of all nationalities. Franklin eventually closed up shop as a result of rising

Atoms.

Auto Helm.

transmission. It did not use a bevel gear. Production ceased at the beginning of the 1990s.

Auto Helm

The Auto Helm trim-tab-on-auxiliary-rudder gear (system type 6) is made in California. Its rustic appearance and the inherent disadvantages of this type of system have prevented it from achieving any more than local recognition. The steering impulse in the Auto Helm gear is transmitted from the windvane to the trim tab via two simple sheathed cables. There is no bevel gear.

The system comes in one size and is marketed by Scanmar International USA.

Auto-Steer

This British company makes two systems (types 8 and 11). An identical

windvane assembly is combined with either a servo-pendulum gear (with bevel gear) or a trim tab system (without bevel gear) attached to the main rudder. Both systems can be obtained from the manufacturer.

Bogasol

The Spanish servo-pendulum gear Bogasol (system type 11) is similar in many ways to the French Navik system: the vane drives a small trim tab at the pendulum rudder without a bevel gear. The rudder can be lifted up at the side.

Bouvaan

This rustic stainless steel servo-pendulum design (type 11) from the Netherlands is aimed particularly at sailors who have the skills required to assemble a system supplied in kit form. If supplied fully assembled, it

Bogasol

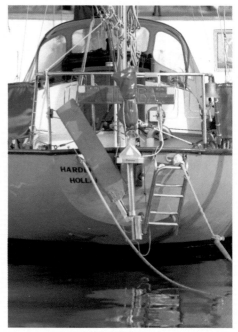

Bouvaan.

is almost as expensive as the visually more attractive professionally built systems.

The system comes in one size and can be obtained directly from the manufacturer.

BWS Taurus

Paul Visser took over this system (type 6) in 1996 after the previous manufacturer, Steenkist, ceased production. The systems are produced one at a time. Neither the auxiliary rudder nor the trim tab can be fixed in the centred position, so the auxiliary rudder will interfere with steering under engine unless removed. The auxiliary rudder on boats whose main rudder is mounted far aft must be removed before manoeuvring under engine for otherwise the two rudders may collide. The transmission ratio of the force from the windvane to the trim tab must be adjusted

BWS Taurus.

manually to prevent the H vane over-steering.

The system is available in three sizes with auxiliary rudder areas of from 0.15 to 0.23 m^2/1$\frac{2}{3}$ to 2$\frac{3}{4}$ ft^2 and is custom built. BWS Taurus systems are some of the most expensive windvane gears available on the world market. They can be obtained directly from the manufacturer.

Cap Horn

The Canadian-built Cap Horn servo-pendulum gear (system type 11) was introduced in the early 1990s. The systems are individually hand-made in stainless steel. The steering line arm of the Cap Horn passes through the transom to the main rudder. This complicates installation because a hole of between 63 and 89 mm/$\frac{1}{4}$ and $\frac{1}{3}$ in has to be drilled in the transom so that the pendulum arm and the steering lines can be mounted inside it (in the stern compartment) and the large hole then has to be very well sealed. Since this method of installation requires a round hole in the vertical plane, it will be necessary to cut an appropriately dimensioned oval hole in a forward- or aft-raked transom. Installing the supporting framework in the stern can be a delicate operation as well, all in all quite a challenge for the DIY owner. Custom-tailored installation components are not part of the standard package.

The idea of keeping the transmission lines off the deck is appealing but turns out not always to be practical. Guiding the lines from the system's quadrant in the stern locker up to deck level often requires quite a few additional turning blocks and a longer transmission path, which together impair the performance of the system. Installation can involve a loss of buoyancy and stowage space at the stern in some boats. The system has no bevel gear and uses two simple 90° bends in the actuating rod to help reset the pendulum rudder; this means, in practical terms, that dropping the servo-rudder in the water during sailing can be difficult because the rudder will not go down on its own. The relatively small power leverage and the dimensions of the windvane and push rod suggest that the range of this system might be limited in terms of boat size.

The Cap Horn does not include a wheel adaptor. The steering lines for wheel steering boats are led around several plastic cylinders mounted on the spokes of the wheel and have to be shortened or lengthened to fine-trim the steering.

Two sizes are available: for boats up to 12 m/40 ft and for boats over 12 m/40 ft. They can be obtained directly from the manufacturer.

Fleming

Australian Kevin Fleming launched his eponymous servo-pendulum system (type 11) in 1974. The distinctive features of the system, besides the bevel gear, were the use of cast stainless steel components and the extension of the pendulum arm up to deck level, which reduced by four the number of turning blocks required. The system was available in three sizes and was relatively expensive. The company closed after a few years. Production was resumed in the mid-1980s by New Zealand Fasteners of Auckland, but sales remained fairly subdued. Kevin Fleming himself moved to San Diego to work on other projects.

Fleming returned to the fray in

1997. The Fleming pendulum system now has a lift-up facility and worm drive remote control, both features known from the Windpilot Pacific. The system is available directly from the manufacturer.

Hydrovane

An auxiliary rudder system (type 4), the Hydrovane is manufactured in England by Derek Daniels. It is available in hand-operated or remote-control versions (VXA 1 and VXA 2) and has changed very little since its introduction in 1970.

The system features a three-position linkage which allows the user to change the effective rudder angle to avoid oversteering. There is no choice of rudder size.

The rudder area amounts to $0.24\,m^2/2\frac{2}{3}\,ft^2$ and the Hydrovane is therefore limited to boats below a

certain critical length. Although the manufacturer specifies the system for boats of up to 15 m / 50 ft (18 tonnes), the lack of servo-assistance would tend to suggest that boats of this size might be too big to be steered effectively in all conditions. The Hydrovane rudder blade is a solid moulded plastic component and therefore has no intrinsic buoyancy. It can be dropped out of the shaft for removal.

Hydrovane systems are built in aluminium using industrial methods and have a good international reputation for their strength and reliability. The overall length and mounting components of the systems are individually tailored to match the particular boat. The range includes:

• VXA 1 system, hand-operated
• VXA 2 system, remote-control

Hydrovane supplies its products directly all over the world.

Fleming.

Hydrovane.

Levanter

This British auxiliary rudder system (types 4 and 10), similar in many details to the Hydrovane, was available in three sizes, and very expensive. Production ceased a few years ago. Levanter recently launched the GS II, a small servo-pendulum system for boats up to 8 m/25 ft. The system can be obtained directly from the manufacturer.

Monitor

Preferring not to return to the cold of their native country at the end of their circumnavigation, Swedes Carl Seipel and Hans Bernwall eventually settled in Sausalito, California. They founded Scanmar Marine in 1978 and have over the years been sales agents for both Sailomat Sweden AB and Navik France. They broke off their association with Sailomat following the high failure rate of the systems in the 1981 Transpac race to Honolulu and the manufacturer's unwillingness to supply spare parts promptly. Since the 1981 Long Beach Boat Show they have had an agreement with Monitor founder Gene Mervin to produce the Monitor gear in-house.

The Monitor (system type 11) is handmade in 319L grade stainless steel. It is very similar to the Aries system and uses an identical bevel gear linkage. Although very well known in the USA, Scanmar only began marketing this system worldwide in 1988.

Although some 20 small improvements have been made, the Monitor is still essentially unchanged from the original design. Hans Bernwall, now the sole proprietor, regards his product as a 'refined' version of the Aries, a gear he refers to respectfully

Monitor.

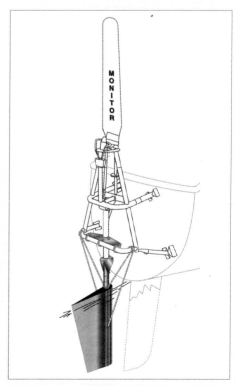

Monitor's emergency rudder conversion kit (MRUD).

as 'Saint Aries'. The Monitor is a traditional windvane steering system and requires a large mounting area on the stern. The steering lines pass through up to ten turning blocks. Installation until 1997 required 16 bolts and individually tailored mounting components made as standard by the manufacturer. Later models will only need 8 bolts fastened to the transom. The fore-and-aft inclination of the windvane cannot be adjusted; the wheel adaptor is adjusted using a track and pin arrangement.

An emergency rudder conversion kit (MRUD) was introduced for the Monitor in 1997. A larger rudder blade with an area of around $0.27\,m^2/2\frac{3}{4}\,ft^2$ is fitted in place of the standard pendulum rudder blade and then the pendulum arm is stabilised in six places with a series of reinforcing measures.

The company enjoys a fine reputation and is renowned for its after-sales support. The Monitor comes in one size for boats of up to about 18 m/60 ft. The system can be seen at all the major European and American boat shows and is distributed by the manufacturer and various sales partners.

Mustafa

The Mustafa, an auxiliary rudder system using a trim tab (type 6), is produced by Italian Franco Malingri. Nowadays, this enormous system is rarely seen. The large area of the rudder blades puts considerable stress on the transom mounting. The system has yaw damping. Weighing up to 60 kg, it is probably the heaviest windvane steering system available.

The Mustafa comes in two sizes:

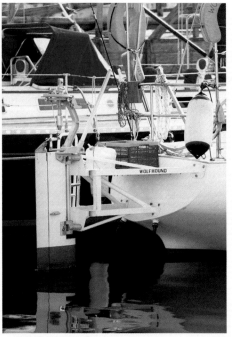

Mustafa.

- B for boats up to 9 m/30 ft
- CE for boats up to 18 m/60 ft.

The systems can be obtained directly from the manufacturer.

Navik

This French servo-pendulum system (type 11), which weighs only 18.5 kg/ $40\frac{1}{2}$ lb, is particularly popular on small boats in its home country. The system is of rather delicate construction and uses plastic linkage components, making it impractical for larger boats. A Super Navik system for larger boats was introduced, but then withdrawn almost immediately. The special feature of the Navik, its lifting pendulum rudder, is not particularly convenient for everyday use since disassembling the axle is very complicated. The windvane is connected to the rudder blade via a small trim tab with delicate plastic ball-and-

Navik.

Super Navik.

socket joints which are quite fragile. The system comes in one size.

The Navik system does not appear at the European boat shows and is available from the manufacturer and from dealers.

RVG

The RVG is another American trim-tab-on-auxiliary-rudder system (type 5). It was built in California until 1977; a former army pilot then took the design to Florida and continued making the systems by hand more or less unchanged. The system has no bevel gear linkage.

The RVG is no longer made.

Sailomat

There has been some confusion in sailing circles regarding the Sailomat name owing to the fact that there were three separate companies using the name at one time. The legal battle between the parties involved lasted for several years and unsettled the market.

Sailomat Sweden AB was founded in 1976 by the three Swedes Boström, Zettergren and Knöös. With financial help from the Swedish treasury, the company developed the Sailomat 3040 double rudder system (system type 12). Elegant and innovative, the design was the first to couple a servo-pendulum system directly to an auxiliary rudder in this way. The system was also tremendously expensive, and fell beyond the reach of many sailors. Exaggerated estimates of the potential market and personal disagreements between the three partners probably contributed to the

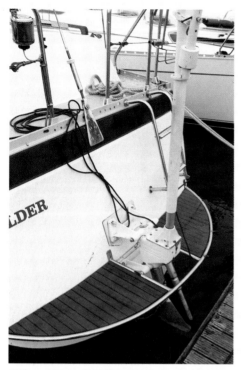

Sailomat/Stayer 3040.

Sailomat 536.

problems of the company. Production ceased in 1981 and the company was dissolved soon after.

H Brinks/Nederland, the former European marketing representative for the company and inheritor of the legal rights to the system, continued to sell off existing stocks for several years. The system was later sold under the name Stayer as a result of legal disputes between the former owners. It finally disappeared from the market at the end of the 1980s.

Sailomat USA was founded by Stellan Knöös in 1984. He designed servo-pendulum systems (type 11) at his base in California and had them manufactured in Sweden.

The Sailomat 500, a hybrid autopilot/windvane system, was launched in 1985. The windvane supplied the steering impulse for on the wind

Sailomat 601.

courses +/− 60° and the autopilot was connected in other cases. The idea failed to catch on and few systems were built.

The Sailomat 536, similar in many ways to the Sailomat 500 but with a 360° windvane, appeared in 1987. The pendulum arm could be raised 90° to one side, which in practical terms actually meant that the rudder had to be removed after use because it would otherwise have stuck out some distance from the side of the boat. Mounting components had to be custom built; variable mounting brackets and remote control were not available.

Next to appear was the Sailomat 600, launched in 1993. A development of the 536, this system had a variable mounting bracket and lift-up facilities – both features known from the Windpilot Pacific.

The Sailomat 601, which appeared in 1996, was similar except that the pendulum arm angle had been modified on this system.

Sailomat systems do not use a bevel gear linkage. Damping is achieved by angling the shaft of the pendulum rudder aft so that the flow of water past the blade slows and damps the lateral movement of the rudder. This angle has been modified a number of times:

Sailomat 3040	= 30°
Sailomat 500	= 15°
Sailomat 536	= 18°
Sailomat 600	= 25°
Sailomat 601	= 34°

The manufacturer recommends further modifying this angle setting (eg by inclining the windvane shaft – whose angle with respect to the pendulum rudder shaft is fixed) to match the damping characteristics to the particular circumstances. This means

accepting a corresponding increase/decrease in the working range of the windvane, because once the shaft is inclined the windvane no longer has an exact amidships position.

The windvane-to-push-rod signal transmission needs to be fine-trimmed manually. A total of 18 settings (six at the windvane combined with three at the linkage) are provided for this purpose. The push rod is designed like a kind of bottlescrew: its effective length changes regularly with every course change when the windvane is adjusted or turned. The operator must be particularly careful here, otherwise frequent course/wind changes may tighten or loosen the screw excessively; the amidships position of the windvane/pendulum rudder is never exactly defined. The wheel adaptor is a fixed drum. Fine adjustments to the course are made by shortening/lengthening the steering lines.

The system is available with different shaft and rudder blade lengths for boats of up to 18 m/60 ft.

The Sailomat gear is present at some of the US boat shows, but is seldom seen at the international shows in Europe. It can be obtained directly from the manufacturer.

Saye's Rig

This American system is a servo-pendulum/trim tab hybrid (type 9). The pendulum rudder is connected underwater to the trailing edge of the main rudder by a long bracket. The bracket transmits lateral movements of the pendulum rudder directly to the main rudder. Damping is provided by the V vane, which is very effective thanks to its wedge-shaped profile.

The Saye's Rig is built in small

numbers in the USA. Depending on the position of the main rudder, the transmission bracket may have to project a long way aft to reach the pendulum rudder. As the two rudders are fixed relative to each other, trim can be adjusted only at the windvane. It is often difficult to move the rudder of a wheel steering system from the wrong end in this way. A bypass valve is not adequate to adapt hydraulic steering systems for the Saye's Rig gear since the oil in the main cylinder still has to be circulated. A bypass valve would also prevent manual steering in the event of an emergency.

Manual steering is only effective once the pendulum system has been disconnected or removed. Owing to the unusual design, this system is suitable for only a few types of boat and main rudder.

The Saye's Rig comes in one size and is available from Scanmar International USA.

Schwingpilot

This German servo-pendulum system (type 10) is built in aluminium using industrial methods and first appeared in 1974. Schwing, an engineering company active mainly in the field of concrete pumps, placed particular emphasis on the possibility of mounting its systems on the pushpit. The gear consequently used a horizontal pendulum arm rather than the conventional vertical arm. The extremely long pendulum arm could be dropped out of its mounting and removed for manoeuvring. As long as the pushpit was stable this system gave good, sensitive steering performance. The course was set using an endless worm gear. Production ceased in 1992.

Windpilot

John Adam founded Windpilot in 1968 after returning from an eventful voyage from England to Cuba aboard a Leisure 17. The story of how, exhausted after days of storms, he ran aground and was arrested by the Cuban military appeared in the press all over the world. He was held for weeks, and it was during this captivity that he finally decided to set up the company.

The following systems were handmade in stainless steel:

System type 3: V vane auxiliary rudder system; model names Atlantik 2/3/4 for boats of up to 8/9/11 m/25/31/35 ft; produced between 1968 and 1985.
System type 5: V vane auxiliary rudder and trim tab system; produced between 1969 and 1971.
System type 10: V vane servo-pendulum system; model name Pacific V; produced between 1970 and 1975.
System type 11: H vane servo-pendulum system; model name Pacific H; produced between 1973 and 1983.
System type 8: H vane trim-tab-on-main-rudder system; model name Pacific; custom produced between 1971 and 1974.

These systems were of very robust construction and most of them are still in use even after the best part of 30 years.

The somewhat unconventional acquisition of the company by the author of this book occurred in 1977. Friends John Adam and Peter C. Förthmann went sailing and agreed a swap: the company for a steel yawl!

Windpilot stopped building its stainless steel systems in 1984–5. The average length of boats equipped

John Adam, founder of Windpilot leaving Weymouth in 1968.

Windpilot Caribic auxiliary rudder
system 1988.

Windpilot Pacific H vane stainless 1974.

with windvane steering had by this time grown to considerably more than 11 m/35 ft.

The all-new Pacific and Pacific Plus twin systems, a state of the art servo-pendulum gear and a double rudder system based on it, were introduced in 1985. With boats getting larger and larger and centre cockpits (which were unfavourable to conventional servo-pendulum systems) becoming increasingly prevalent, this synthesis of the advantages of an auxiliary rudder gear with those of a servo-pendulum system proved to be the logical answer.

The Pacific and Pacific Plus designs have changed very little since their launch. They have all the features of a modern servo-pendulum system: infinitely adjustable; easy to remove; H windvane; infinite remote control; bevel gear linkage for automatic yaw damping; lift-up pendulum rudder; adjustable mounting components; short transmission paths; infinitely adjustable wheel adaptor with a universal mounting flange for all wheel steering systems; low weight; compact modular construction in AlMg 5 grade aluminium alloy. The systems are manufactured using industrial sand casting and diecasting methods and then machined on modern 5 axis CNC equipment.

Both systems won prizes for their avant-garde design and have been exhibited at the German Museum for Art and Design. The novel features of the systems are legally protected by German patent P 36 14 514.9–22.

Windpilot Pacific Light (1996).

Windpilot Pacific (1985-1997).

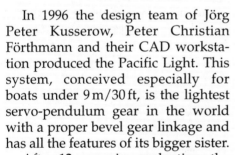

Windpilot Pacific Plus.

Windpilot Pacific (1998).

In 1996 the design team of Jörg Peter Kusserow, Peter Christian Förthmann and their CAD workstation produced the Pacific Light. This system, conceived especially for boats under 9 m/30 ft, is the lightest servo-pendulum gear in the world with a proper bevel gear linkage and has all the features of its bigger sister.

After 12 years in production, the Pacific and Pacific Plus twin systems came up for fundamental overhaul in 1997–8. The new Pacific, although identical in its technical features to the older model, now has a multi-functional mounting system which makes it even more straightforward to install on all kinds of transoms. The flange cheeks now adapt to follow the curve of the transom easily, a feature that removes the need for wooden spacers between hull and flange and prevents any kind of strain at flange or hull side. The Pacific Plus, in turn, now has a 'Quick-in, Quick-out' linkage which allows the pendulum rudder to be engaged with/disengaged from the auxiliary rudder even under load. This should simplify operation of the system considerably for the average sailor. Since the linkage can be operated one-handed, it is possible to simultaneously disengage the pendulum rudder and fix the auxiliary rudder on the centreline. Both systems now have a practical device for locking the windvane in its centred position and provide means for connecting an Autohelm cockpit autopilot. The change in the manufacturing process from sand casting to diecasting, the technique now favoured in industry, ensures perfect cast components with a highly smooth surface and even greater precision.

Windpilot Pacific (1998 model) multifunctional mounting system.

Windpilot plans to introduce a double rudder system for boats of 18–23 m/60–75 ft sometime in 1998.

Windpilot has been around now for over 30 years and is probably the world's oldest surviving manufacturer of windvane steering systems. It is certainly the only one currently offering a complete range of modular systems for all types of boat.

The range includes:

- System type 11: Pacific Light for boats less than 9 m/30 ft
- System type 11: Pacific for boats less than 18 m/60 ft
- System type 12: Pacific Plus I for boats less than 12 m/40 ft
- System type 12: Pacific Plus II for boats less than 18 m/60 ft

Windpilot systems are marketed worldwide and are supplied directly by the manufacturer. The company is represented at all the major European boat shows. A US subsidiary based in Florida maintains the company's presence at the major US and Canadian shows.

Windtrakker

This English manufacturer recently launched a servo-pendulum system (type 11) which resembles the Aries in even the smallest details. Time will tell whether copies such as this will survive in the market even when the original is available at a better price.

The system can be obtained directly from the manufacturer.

Appendix:
Systems Manufacurers

Autopilots

Alpha

Alpha Marine Systems
1235 Columbia Hill Road
Reno, NV 89506
USA
Tel: ++1 800 257 4225

Autohelm

Raytheon Electronics
Anchorage Park
Portsmouth
Hants PO3 5TD
UK
Tel: ++44 1705 69 36 11
Fax: ++44 1705 69 46 42

Raytheon Marine Company
46 River Road
Hudson NH 03051
USA

Factory Service Center
Raytheon Marine Company
1521 SO 92nd Place
Seattle WA 98108
USA
Tel: ++1 206 763 7500

Benmar

Cetec Benmar
3320 W MacArthurr Blvd
Santa Ana CA 92704
USA
Tel: ++1 714 540 5120
Fax:++1 714 641 2614

Brookes & Gatehouse

Brookes & Gatehouse Ltd UK
Premier Way, Abbey Park
Romsey
Hants SO51 9AQ
UK
Tel: ++44 1794 51 84 48
Fax: ++44 1794 51 80 77
Website: www.bandg.co.uk

Brookes & Gatehouse USA
7855 126th Avenue North
Suite B
Largo FL 33773 USA
Tel: ++1 813 530 1213
Fax: ++1 813 530 1704

Cetrek

Cetrek UK
1 Factory Road
Upton
Poole BH16 5SJ
UK
Tel: ++44 1202 63 21 16
Fax: ++44 1202 63 19 80

Cetrek USA
640 North Lewis Road
Limerick
PA 19468
USA
Tel: ++1 610 495 0671
Fax: ++1 610 495 0675
Website: www.cetrek.co.uk

Coursemaster

Coursemaster USA INC
232 Richardson
Greenpoint
NY 11222 USA
Tel: ++1 718 383 4968
Fax: ++1 718 383 1864

Navico

Navico Ltd UK
Star Lane
Margate, Kent CT9 4NP
UK
Tel: ++44 1843 29 02 90
Fax: ++44 1843 29 04 71

Navico Inc USA
11701 Belcher Road Suite 128
Largo, FL 34643 USA
Tel: ++1 813 524 1555
Fax: ++1 813 524 1355

Robertson

Simrad Robertson AS
PO Box 55
N 4371 Egersund
Norway
Tel: ++47 51 46 20 00
Fax: ++47 51 46 20 01
Web site: www.simrad.com

Segatron

Gerhard Seegers
Bleichenstr 73
D-31515 Wunstorf, Germany
Tel: ++49 5033 1660
Fax: ++49 5033 2066

Silva

Silva Sweden AB
Kuskvägen 4
S 19162 Sollentuna
Sweden
Tel: ++46 8 623 43 00
Fax: ++46 8 92 76 01
Web site: www.silva.s

VDO

VDO Kienzle GmbH
Rüsselsheimerstr 22
60326 Frankfurt, Germany
Tel: ++49 69 75860
Fax: ++49 69 7586210

Vetus

Vetus Den Ouden Ltd
38 South Hants Ind Park
Totton, Southampton SO40 3SA
UK
Tel: ++44 1703 86 10 33
Fax: ++44 1703 66 31 42

Vetus Den Ouden USA Inc
PO Box 8712
Baltimore, Maryland 21240
USA
Tel: ++1 410 712 0740

W – H

W – H Autopilots Inc
150 Madrone Lane North
Bainbridge Island, WA 98110-1863
USA
Tel: ++1 206 780 2175
Fax: ++1 206 780 2186

Windhunter

Windhunter
82 Great Eastern Street
London EC2A 3JL
UK
Tel: ++44 181 500 0180
Fax: ++44 181 500 5100

MOB systems
Emergency Guard

Jonathan GMBH
Usedomstr 14
22047 Hamburg, Germany
Tel: ++49 40 66 97 67 40
Fax: ++49 40 66 97 67 49
Mobile:++45 405 81 953

Windvane steering systems
Aries (spare parts for all existing systems)

Aries Spares Helen Franklin
48 St Thomas Street
Penryn, Cornwall TR10 8JW
UK
Tel: ++44 1326 377467
Fax: ++44 1326 378117

Aries Standard

Peter Matthiesen
Mollegade 54, Holm
DK 6430 Nordborg, Denmark
Tel: ++45 74 45 0760
Fax: ++45 74 45 2960

Auto Helm

Scanmar International
432 South 1st Street
Richmond CA 94804-2107
USA
Tel: ++1 510 2152010
Fax: ++1 510 2155005
E-mail: selfsteer @ aol.com

Auto-Steer

Clearway Design
3 Chough Close
Tregoniggie Ind Estate
Falmouth, Cornwall TR11 4SN
UK

Tel: ++44 1326 376048
Fax: ++44 1326 376164

Bogasol

Egui Diseny
Calle Provensa 157 bis
E 08036 Barcelona, Spain
Tel: ++34 3 451 18 79

Bouvaan

Tjeerd Bouma
Brahmsstraat 57
NL 6904 DB Zevenaar
Nederland
Tel: ++31 8360 25566

BWS

Taurus Scheepsbouw & Uitrusting
Nijverheidstraat 16
NL 1521 NG Wormerveer, Nederland
Tel: ++31 75 640 33 62
Fax: ++31 75 640 26 21

Cap Horn

Cap Horn
316 avenue Girouard
OKA JON 1EO, Canada
Tel: ++1 514 4796314
Fax: ++1 514 4791895

Fleming

Fleming Marine USA Inc
3724 Dalbergia Street
San Diego CA 92113
USA
Tel: ++1 619 557 0488
Fax: ++1 619 557 0476

Levanter

Levanter Marine Equipment
Gandish Road
East Bergholt, Colchester CO7 6UR
UK
Tel: ++44 1206 298242

Hydrovane

Hydrovane Yacht Equipment Ltd
117 Bramcote Lane
Chilwell, Nottingham NG9 4EU
UK
Tel: ++44 115 925 6181
Fax: ++44 115 943 1408

Monitor

Scanmar International
432 South 1st Street
Richmond CA 94804-2107 USA
Tel: ++1 510 215 2010
Fax: ++1 510 215 5005
E-mail: selfsteer @ aol.com
Web site: www.selfsteer.com

Mustafa

EMI SRI
Via Lanfranchi 12
I 25036 Palazzolo
Italy
Tel/Fax: ++39 30 7301438

Navik

Plastimo France
15 rue Ingénieur Verrière
F 56325 Lorient
France
Tel: ++33 2 97 87 36 36
Fax: ++33 2 97 87 36 49

RVG

International Marine
Manufacturing Co
8895 SW 129 Street
Miami FL 33176
USA
Tel/Fax: ++1 305 255 3939

Sailomat

POBox 2077
La Jolla Californien CA 92038
USA
Tel: ++1 619 454 6191
Fax: ++1 619 454 3512

Saye's Rig

Scanmar International
432 South 1st Street
Richmond CA 94804-2107
USA
Tel: ++1 510 2010
Fax: ++1 510 215 5005
E-mail: selfsteer@aol.com

Windpilot

Windpilot
Bandwirkerstrasse 39–41
D-22041 Hamburg, Germany
Tel: ++49 40 652 52 44
Fax: ++49 40 68 65 15
Mobile: ++49 172 401 33 80
E-mail: windpilot@t-online.de
Web site: www.windpilot.com

Windpilot USA

PO Box 8565
Madeira Beach, FL 33738
USA
Tel: ++1 813 319 8017
Fax: ++1 813 398 6288
Toll free:++1 888 Windpilot
E-mail: windpilot@compuserve.com

Windtrakker

Trakker Marine Ltd
Island Farm Avenue
West Molesey, Surrey KT8 2UW
UK
Tel: ++44 181 979 8491
Fax: ++44 181 941 7457
Bielefeld, Germany.

Index

A Robertson autopilot never gets tired or bored. It replaces the helmsman who then can share his time between watch keeping and boating pleasure. An alarm will warn you if your present heading exceeds a preset limit.

SIMRAD MARKETING 11.97

Robertson AP20 Autopilot - Straight Forward Quality

The Robertson AP20 Autopilot continues the tradition in autopilot making that has been awarded by the NMEA in 12 consecutive years. With the new Simrad MarineLine design and software that enhances the user interface, the AP20 offers new standards in autopilot performance.

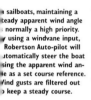

n sailboats, maintaining a steady apparent wind angle is normally a high priority. By using a windvane input, Robertson Auto-pilot will automatically steer the boat using the apparent wind angle as a set course reference. Wind gusts are filtered out to keep a steady course.

Use the rotary course knob to set your course which is clearly read on the display.

Minor course adjustments are made in one degree increments by a single press on the port or starboard key.

In navigation mode the autopilot receives signals from the chart plotter or GPS navigator about present position, cross track error (XTE) and distance to the waypoint.

While keeping the boat on track, a warning is given when you are within the waypoint arrival circle. Then displaying the next waypoint name and course, it prompts you to acknowledge the course change for safety reasons.

Simrad MarineLine™

Wind and current may off-set the boat from a track even if it maintains the set course (1). The cross track error (XTE) is continuously calculated by the navigator or plotter and transferred to the auto-pilot which then counteracts the effect of wind and current and keeps the boat on track (2).

Integration of marine electronic equipment into user-friendly, attractive looking systems is a requisite for the discerning yacht owner. The well known brands Robertson and Shipmate are wholly incorporated with Simrad - the world-wide manufacturer of marine electronics. Offering the ultimate solution for fishfinding, steering, communication and navigation -the Simrad MarineLine.™

ptimizing steering performance to the speed of the boat is made automatically by log or GPS input, or manually by a quick push button operation.

In addition to the primary functions, the Robertson AP20 Autopilot acts as an instrument repeater, ideally complementing any NMEA 0183 compatible instrument system.

or a free brochure and a list of Simrad dealers near you, call: Simrad, Inc. Tel: (425) 778-8821.
ax: (425) 771-7211 19210 33rd Ave. We. Lynnwood, WA 98036 USA

SIMRAD
A KONGSBERG Company

WORLDWIDE MANUFACTURER OF MARINE ELECTRONICS

Autohelm
Autopilots

From the first name in autopilots, the last word in choice.

When it comes to selecting an autopilot, skippers agree that Autohelm is the only serious choice.

That's because we make the world's most comprehensive range of autopilots, from the economical yet powerful AH 800 Plus to the top-of-the-range ST 7000.

Whether you have a power or sail craft, wheel or tiller steering, and whatever the size and displacement, there is an Autohelm autopilot to match.

Little wonder, then, that Autohelm is the world's most widely chosen autopilot, with thousands of satisfied users around the globe. And glowing magazine reviews and customer testimonials that confirm the reliability and excellence of our products.

Yet we never rest on our laurels. Last year we introduced the Autohelm Plus range, with superb new displays, elegant styling, new back lit buttons and excellent night lighting. Whatever craft you have, there's an Autohelm autopilot for you.

Add to that our unrivalled warranty backup and comprehensive worldwide after-sales service, and one thing becomes clear.

The choice name in autopilots is Autohelm.

ST 600R

ST 6000 Plus

ST 7000

ST 6000

24 HR BROCHURE HOTLINE
01705 655811

Raytheon Marine Company
Recreational Products
Anchorage Park
Portsmouth, Hampshire
England PO3 5TD
Telephone (01705) 693611
Fax (01705) 694642
www.raytheon.com

Raytheon Marine Company
Recreational Products
676 Island Pond Road
Manchester
NH 03109-5420, USA
Telephone 603.647.7530
Fax 603.634.4756
www.raytheon.com

Raytheon

WINDPILOT ®

...because wind is the better pilot

German technology

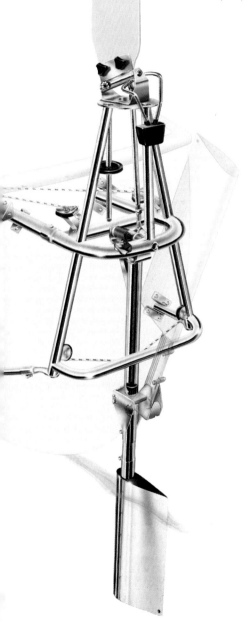